I0140369

Single Steps In A Married World

Stepping Out of the Shadows of Codependency, Complacency & Insecurity

Aaron Publishing
Shelbyville, TN 37160

1

Single Steps In A Married World

Stepping Out of the Shadows of Codependency, Complacency & Insecurity

By:

ANN HANEY

www.annhaney.com

Printed in the United States of America

First Printing, March 2014

ISBN 978-0-9916077-1-6

Published by
Aaron Publishing
225 Peacock Lane
Shelbyville, TN 37160
www.aaronpublishing.com

Dedication

This book is dedicated to all women who are single, married, separated, divorced or widowed. As women we all share a common bond and that is the desire to love and be loved. The heart of a woman cries out to nurture, admonish and make this world a better place, leaving behind a legacy that impacts future generations with hope and love. Through tears she pushes on knowing that her work is not in vain. Through laughter she changes the atmosphere. Through a tender smile she offers peace to a conflicting environment and an anxious soul. The life of a woman is far from easy yet far from insignificant. Her journey is often scarred by the pain of loneliness, misunderstanding and often contempt. But one thing remains and that is love. She understands its value, and through humble patience she endures life's journey with a smile laying down her life for those she loves. Her motto is "a life worth living requires self-sacrifice." She trusts God without end, hopes beyond her vision and loves beyond her disappointments.

"Three things will last forever--faith, hope, and love--and the greatest of these is love."
1 Corinthians 13:13

Foreward

Over the past year my heart has become painfully aware of the severe sense of inadequacy many women face. In their search to be happy they have found an inability to feel confident and yet they continue to strive towards a sense of completeness. I have been approached by many women who are divorced and while they strive to learn independence and stability their hearts cry out with brokenness and insecurity. This insecurity not only attacks the divorced woman, but the single, married, separated and widowed. For the single woman it is a longing for completion. For the married woman it is a desire for oneness and unity. For the separated woman it is the struggle to regain purpose and value. For the divorced woman, it is a journey to recover confidence. Finally, the widowed woman searches for the strength to live again. Insecurity and low self-esteem are truly the biggest enemy to our society of women today.

When value and purpose have been stripped away, all that is left is an empty shell. For the weary, depression, regret, confusion and desperation often set in. It troubles me greatly to see women who have gone so far to desperately grasp worthiness that they compromise their bodies for acceptance. Society is filled with hurting women we view as prostitutes, yet they are really prodigals who have given up on purpose and turned to reckless living. Their hearts are tainted with a painful past and present that have sent them looking for every human's desire and that is to be loved. Prostitutes do not only exist on the streets, but also behind closed doors within marriages.

We must identify this attack on women and expose it for what it is—an attempt to break down who they are and who they're called to be. We must understand that the real enemy is not man, but Satan and the manipulative mindsets he places on man.

Every woman must set out on this journey in search of her identity with disregard to those who strive to tear down her purpose. No man can give her identity, only God. For some, the support of a companion adds strength in her journey.

For others, they are but single steps in a married world. The ability to overcome the enemy's intended destruction lies not in the marital oneness of the couple, but in the individual's discovery of who they are in Christ.

In this book I will prove through what I have experienced and heard from other women that we are capable of the victory and able to regain what has been lost, our value and purpose. You see, we are daughters of the most High King, capable, honored, loved, nurtured and worthy.

"A capable, intelligent and virtuous woman—who is he who can find her? She is far more precious than jewels and her value is far above rubies or pearls."
Proverbs 31:10

My prayer for you as you read this book is that no matter who or where you are now or where you've been, you'll discover the woman God sees in you today. May your chains of bondage be broken as you walk in God's purpose for your life, experiencing the freedom you were meant to have.

"The Spirit of the Lord God is upon me because the Lord has anointed and qualified me to preach the Gospel of good tidings to the meek, the poor and afflicted. He has sent me to bind up and heal the broken hearted, to proclaim liberty to the (physical and spiritual) captives and open the prison and of the eyes to those who are bound."
Isaiah 61:1

May the journey of restoration begin in you today, Woman of God!

Introduction

On the following pages you will be get an inside look at the struggles many women face with insecurity and low self-esteem. We see many women who often wear a mask of self-confidence, but who below the surface are suffering from self-doubt and lack of purpose. For some women this was planted in them at childhood, for others life's situations changed their focus of who they are and what they can be. Far too many women who find themselves victimized by with self-confidence issues become easy targets for abusive relationships, further increasing their low self-esteem. The goal of this book is not to point fingers at anyone or anything, but rather to understand the tactics of the enemy and how to diffuse his plan by bringing God's word to life in the reader. For every negative circumstance, God has a positive word of reassurance to help the imprisoned overcome through perseverance, faith and love.

Women not only long to discover happiness and find their purpose, but to secure the futures of their children. The fear of failure at raising stable children when she herself feels unstable is often the strongest cry of the woman's heart. She has an overwhelming desire to change the course of her child's life even when hers seems less than perfect.

It is love that breaks the yoke of bondage in every relationship. It mends her hurting heart, secures the steps of her children and shows forth Christ to those who see her as their enemy. The love of Christ can be present in the life of a woman even when human love is impossible. For Christ loves the sick as much as He does the well and His love is stronger than any human love will ever be.

As you read this book, I pray you will open your mind and heart to allow God to speak to you and meet your needs, directing your paths into His perfect plan for your life. Let Him search your heart and sort the wheat from the chaff creating within you His purpose for your life and your relationships with others. Remember this one thing as you begin: *"For all have sinned and come short of the Glory of God."*
Romans 3:23

Contents

Chapter 1

Power of the Past

"*Uncovering the Strongholds*"

The power of love is greatly underestimated in its importance in the life of a human being. Furthermore we often do not understand how crucial it is in shaping a child's life and how the lack of love can completely change a child's future and ability to interact with others positively. It has been discovered that a person's character is mostly shaped by the age of five. This is not to say that what occurs in a person's life at other stages does not greatly impact their outlook on love and acceptance. However, a child's first look at love and discovering its impact on his or her emotions and safety is from birth to five years old. These are also the crucial ages when a child develops emotions such as fear, independence, anger, happiness and more. They began to imitate what they see their parents doing and perceive it as normal behavior. This shows us the crucial role a parent's life has on that of a child. It can be a time when either rejection or acceptance is first experienced by a child and thus becomes a part of the child's makeup and expectations. It's interesting that at the young age of 1-2 years old a child begins to direct the way others interact with them based upon what they have learned firsthand.[1]

Let's take a deeper look into what this means in the life of an adult. Many women today are influenced by what has been implanted in them during childhood. Although they may grow up to be responsible adults there are generally trigger points for feelings like insecurity and rejection that might be easily surfaced through the words or actions of others. For example, a child who grows up without the presence of a father figure will often feel a sense of incompleteness or wondering who they really are. Many women who grew up without the absence of a father figure do not know what the love of man should resemble and are therefore vulnerable to almost any behavior as acceptable. This can often lead to many failed relationships or unhappy marriages. This also affects a woman who does not have a positive mother figure in her life. She has learned a false sense of what a mother should be like. In either sense, although the woman may know the behavior of the parent was improper, they

[1] http://psychology.about.com/od/early-child-development/a/social-and-emotional-milestones.htm

cannot break free from its negative impact on their lives. The same thing happens in the life of a man. A man whose father treats his mother with contempt or speaks negatively of women will likely do the same. Just as a man whose mother fails to nurture her son and spends her life self- consumed, he will tend to have a negative view of a wife and mother.

Love is crucial to a person's life. After all we were made in love with the commission to love others. Love is proven to alleviate stress, heal wounds and increase brain productivity. Studies show that those who experience high levels of stress produce more of the hormone cortisol. Cortisol suppresses the immune system leaving the body vulnerable to colds, flu, etc.. It also causes the body to store fat around abdominal organs and has been linked to heart disease, cancer and diabetes. A study was done to see if the presence of more love and less stress could actually stimulate healing at an Ohio State University. Researchers found through a blistering procedure that couples who engaged in supportive communication and behavior as opposed to provoking tension healed two days quicker than those who did not. Furthermore couples in midlife who experienced love had a lower risk for poor memory and mental functioning.[1] Therefore, if love is proven to positively affect the functions of the body, the lack of love will have a negative effect on a person's overall well-being.

Often, our comfort zone seems to be in what we have been taught to believe is truth, when in fact it is bondage to improper thinking about who we are. Is it possible to flee from our past never to be challenged with it again?" Unfortunately, the answer is no. However, just because it is a part of your life doesn't mean it has to control any of your life. We make a decision at the point of conflict to ride above the storm and let God lead or go it alone and face the consequences of defeat.

In the case of Lot's wife who was turned to a pillar of salt as she lingered and looked back to Sodom and Gomorrah, we see how living in the past, even in her

[1]http://health.yahoo.net/experts/dayinhealth/
surprisinghealth-
benefits-love

heart and mind, brought complete destruction to her life.

"When morning came, the angels urged Lot to hurry...lest you (too) be consumed and swept away in iniquity and punishment of the city...But, while he lingered, the men seized him and his wife and two daughters by the hand, for the Lord was merciful to him and they brought them forth and set them outside the city and left them there...And when they had brought them forth they said, 'Escape for your life! Do not look behind you or stop anywhere...lest you be consumed....but Lot's wife looked back from behind him, and she became a pillar of salt.'"
Genesis 19:15-17,26

There is a very important message in this for women. The past can have such a draw on us that we have a hard time staying forward focused. We will often look back to what we have lived and learned to deal with instead of stepping out into where God is leading us. Notice that even though they had been led outside of their situation and given direction, Lot's wife did not escape, but was consumed as she held on to the past and its familiarity.

What has God shown you that He wants you to do? Who has He placed in your path to lead you out? There are two very special women who God has placed in my life who have helped lead me out from behind the prison of mental bondage, which had for many years kept me chained to a life void of purpose and calling. My dreams and ambitions had always been filled with self-doubt until these women began to push me toward what I knew in my heart was God's calling for my life. Just as the men could not make Lot's wife go forward, others can only advise you. It is up to you to follow through to victory, letting go of the past hurts, comforts, mistakes and strongholds.

I want to show you an example of how my past self-doubt had an impact on my life years ago. As a young adult I learned that I had been adopted and that my biological father was not the father I now knew. Meeting with him brought to surface fears that I was not a daughter he would be proud of or one he would want as part of his life. Although these insecurities had been present in me since birth, they now became a real part of my life that I sought to control. In fact, this was the case in my situation after meeting him. He informed me his life had been pre-established for many years and my curiosity was to be pacified by this one meeting. My search to be a better person, one worthy of love, began with trying to prove my worth in a worldly sense. I mistakenly thought that if I could be thinner, prettier, smarter, a better mother and wife than I could somehow regain my worth. This led to a vicious cycle of eating disorders bouncing from anorexia to bulimia and eventually leading to two surgeries, a Tonsillectomy and a Cholecystectomy. I found myself struggling with depression and anti-depressants as well as over-the-counter medications for every symptom to mask the pain of rejection.

What many women fail to realize is that this insecurity and lack of self-worth sets them up for physical, mental and sexual abuse inflicted by themselves or by companions. In the case of a companion abuser, women have such a low self-esteem that they begin to think they are always the problem and allow themselves to be beaten down adding to their self-esteem deficiency. They will often think others would be happier if they did not exist. Sometimes they are told as much. Low self-esteem opens women up to vulnerability to abuse and is hard to break free from.

In 1996 I attended a Joyce Meyer conference and my life was changed forever. I received the Holy Spirit in fullness of power, even though I had been saved since the age of thirteen. At this conference I discovered my worth in Christ and learned that I had been victimized by Satan for many years letting him convince me that I had no purpose. This revelation through the Holy Spirit's power was the first step to my healing.

"I knew you before I formed you in your mother's womb. Before you were born I set you apart and appointed you as my prophet to the nations."
Jeremiah 1:5

God had delivered me from the

strongholds of doubt and reassured me that He had planned my existence and had a purpose for it, just as He has a purpose for you. Although I now knew the truth, this did not mean I would never face the struggle to overcome mental anguish. But, this time I knew who I was and battled to hold my ground as a daughter of the King.

Choices will always lie before us as to what we allow ourselves to believe. It is true that our choices can help or hurt our relationships with others. We can choose to become more than who we were raised to believe we are or who we have been told we are. I don't know too many who have a spotless past and a perfect childhood, but I do know many, including myself, who have struggled with the impacts of a less than perfect past.

How do we deal with the pain and the uprising of words and actions that stimulate our negative pasts? First, we must give our past to God completely! By completely, I mean surrendering your ability to control the outcome and trusting Him to carry you through the challenge.

New ground should never be viewed as a tombstone, but rather a stepping stone. God will never lead you where He has not empowered you to achieve victory. Pray hard and pray often. Be on a hotline to God at all times. When your emotions well up, let your prayers rise up. Quote this verse frequently:

"Do not be conformed to this world, but be transformed (changed) by the (entire) renewal of your mind (by its new ideals and new attitude), so that you may prove (for yourselves) what is the good and acceptable and perfect will of God, even the thing which is good and acceptable and perfect (in His sight for you.)

Romans 12:2

Second, have a good support system, but be careful in choosing them. Not everyone will understand your challenge. A good friend will speak positive words of encouragement, but will also admonish you to strive for victory. They will lead you outside the past and face you toward the future in confidence. Their words will empathize with you, but not pity you. A good friend is expecting a victory from you. Let me encourage you not to share with too many your struggles. Be led by the Lord. Many times a good Christian counselor is worth the investment. They will listen and advise you on how to overcome the difficulties you face. Let me also say, that everyone faces challenge and no one is exempt from heartache. We all need a shoulder to cry on from time to time. The first step to complete emotional healing is humbly admitting you need it and that you need to be refueled on a regular basis. Seeing a counselor should never be viewed as a weakness, but rather wisdom. It is the humble who receive victory not those who go it alone.

"Without good direction, people lose their way; the more wise counsel you follow, the better your chances."
Proverbs 11:14

Prayer is the fuel for the soul and praise is the prerequisite to victory. Both will keep you at your best.

"Do not be anxious about anything, but in everything by prayer and supplication

with thanksgiving let your requests be made known to God. And the peace of God, which surpasses all understanding, will guard your hearts and your minds in Christ Jesus."
Philippians 4:6-7

In light of all this we understand how strong the past can be on our present. It is important to do a little digging to discover how you were raised, what you were taught to accept as truth and how relationships were to be viewed in regards to your interaction with others. Doing this will allow you to begin to pinpoint where your insecurities and struggle with low self-esteem may be coming from. The first step must always be to identify why you think the way you think.

Once you have uncovered the root of the problem mentalities, the battle heats up as Satan strives to keep you in mental, physical, emotional and spiritual bondage. In the next chapter I will discuss how knowledge of who you are places you on the battlefield to becoming who you were meant to be. But, the good news is this– You were created to win and win you will!

Chapter 2

Identity Crisis

"*Seeing Yourself Through God's Eyes*"

Identity is referred to as the distinct personalities and characteristics which make up a person. When God created mankind He said it was good! Each individual was as unique and valued as another.

"Before I shaped you in the womb....I had Holy plans for you."
Jeremiah 1:5

You were not a surprise to God. Your birth may not have been planned, maybe you were born out of wedlock, possibly the outcome of a rape or maybe even the child of a failed abortion. God does not see you through the eyes of a mistake, but rather knew you before you were born, had prepared your future and rejoiced in the day you would arrive to begin the great work He had for you to glorify His name.

An identity that is in captivity is the condition of a child of God who does not understand what unconditional love of the Father is and what it means for their life. Let's take a look at a situation in King David's life which so clearly displays what captivity can do to someone and what is required to be set free. In 1 Samuel 30 we see the following situation unfold:

"Now when David and his men came home to Ziklag...they found that the Amalekites had made a raid...and had taken the women and all who were there, both great and small, captive. They killed no one, but carried them off and went on their way. Then David and his men came to the town and behold, it was burned and their wives and sons and daughters were taken captive. Then David and the men with him lifted up their voices and wept until they had no more strength to weep. David was greatly distressed for the men spoke of stoning him because the souls of them all were bitterly grieved....But David encouraged and strengthened himself in the Lord his God. David said to Abiathar, the priest...I pray you bring me the ephod. And David inquired of the Lord saying, Shall I pursue this troop? Shall I overtake them? The Lord answered him, Pursue, for you shall surely overtake them and without fail recover all."
1 Sam. 30:3-4,6,7-8

Notice the following key factors that take place in a situation of captivity:

1. Captivity knows no age.
(The enemy will steal the future of anyone and everyone he can in attempts to bring defeat.)
2. Captivity will control your direction.
(The women were all carried away from their homes in a direction they did not wish to go. Although they were not killed, the enemy can steer us off the course of where God has predestined us to be.)
3. Captivity creates anger, exhaustion, blame and pain.
(David and his men wept in loud voices until they had no more strength. When exhaustion set in, anger and blame began to be cast upon David. There was talk of stoning him because of their pain. Many times in pain we look for an explanation to alleviate the feeling of failure that grips us so tightly. This happens with both men and women. An abused woman will often be so emotionally broken that bitterness and blame for her situation can be cast upon her abuser. For the abuser, a failure in himself can often be a reason for lash

ing out against his companion in attempt to regain a sense of control over his own life and shift ownership of the problem onto his mate. Both are wrong mentalities and I will discuss them more in a later chapter.

How did David turn this situation around and regain the position God wanted for his family and gain victory? He did several things:

1. Increased his trust in God
(He encouraged himself and strengthened himself in God. He knew God's track record of goodness to him and knew God would restore peace as He had so many times before. The first place to look in restoring identity is to God in confident assurance that He is who says He is and does what no one else can do, deliver victory.)
2. Consulted God
(David called for the priest to bring the ephod, this was done whenever he sought to question God regarding something, so he could ask for God's direction. In this book you will see the pain and captivity of many women expressed. What you will

not find is the answer to your specific situation and directions for you to take. I believe the ultimate answer and perfect direction for each individual can only be found by each woman consulting God to discover His purpose and plan for her. What I will show you is that victory is always assured when God is in control and you walk in His footsteps for you. Notice David did not call a board meeting and take a vote on what should be done, he took his questions before the Lord, as each woman must do. It matters not what everyone else believes you should do, only God.)

It is important to note King David asked two questions and received three answers. God covers the bases we tend to leave out. David asked:
    1. Do I go?
    2. Will I overcome?
God replied:
    1. Go
    2. You will overcome
    3. You will recover all

"Now to Him Who, by (in consequence of) the [action of His] power that is at work

within us, is able to [carry out His purpose and] do superabundantly, far over and above all that we [dare] ask or think [infinitely beyond our highest prayers, desires, thoughts, hopes, or dreams]"
Ephesians 3:20

I want to take this journey with David a little farther to show you what is often involved in recovering what has been taken captive.

"David went, he and the six hundred men with him. They arrived at the Brook Besor, where some of them dropped out... Some who went on came across an Egyptian in a field and took him to David....David said who do you belong to? Where are you from?....David said can you take us to the raiders?...David pounced...He fought them before sunrise until evening...David rescued everything the Amalakites had taken...Nothing and no one was missing...David recovered the whole lot."
1 Samuel 30:9, 11-15, 17

David's journey took action, perseverance and the ability to identify opportunity when it presented itself. David:

1. Set out to recover what had been taken.

(Are you ready to regain your identity and take back the confidence that has been stolen from you and removed you from the call on your life?)

2. Persevered even when others dropped out of the tiresome journey.

(Are you ready to push on to victory when others say you can't make it or it means going on alone?)

3. Saw the opportunity that would lead him to what had been taken from him.

(Do you know what it is you're called to do, yet allow the opportunities to slip by because of fear of failure or condemnation? This can be especially hard for the codependent woman who puts all her security in her companion, with the belief that she can't do it alone if her mate is unsupportive. If you are this woman, let me remind you that God created you for an individual purpose as well. Your ability does not depend on your relationships stability. If you have been plagued with comments like:

"You'll never succeed without me"
"I got you where you are"
"You're neglecting your family"
"How can God use you?"
"You are so Holy (in sarcasm)"

These types of remarks are made to bring doubt and insecurity into the life of a woman. Guilt is used in regards to her family, especially her children in an attempt to keep her codependent. God has clearly lined out the roles of a Godly woman in Proverbs 31 and she is well-equipped to be a multitasker, caring for the family, the needy and investing in herself and her calling. Sarcasm is often used in regards to her spirituality trying to instill a lack of confidence in what she believes she has heard from God. When this doesn't work, the past is often brought up in attempts to show her weaknesses and instill doubt in her ability to overcome. Remarks of the abuser's accomplishments and contribution to her success will always come up as a way to demean her as an individual. This places her as a dependent rather than a vessel for God's glory.

When your identity is based on the approval of a man your mind becomes enslaved to doubt & your vision remains clouded. Women who know who they are in Christ despite the hurtful words of others become complete and develop strength to change their future. God's plan for your life is this:

"For I know the plans I have for you," declares the Lord, "plans to prosper you and not harm you, plans to give you hope and a future."
Jeremiah 29:11

What is your identity "Woman of God?"

"...You are a chosen race, a royal priesthood, a dedicated nation, [God's] own purchased, special people, that you may set forth the wonderful deeds and display the virtues and perfections of Him who called you out of darkness into His marvelous light."
1 Peter 2:9

Chapter 3

Marrying Your Maker

"Footprints in Sinking Sand"

In the next chapter we will take a look at five categories of women and how "Marrying Their Maker" transformed their lives.

When the heartache of unworthiness plagues your mind as a woman, it is a struggle to find value despite your marital status. The steps you take seem to weigh you down with a longing for something more. Although your daily routines keep you in a forward motion, the heaviness of your steps seems to bury you beneath the hurt as you drag through one more day. It often reminds me of treading water only to be knocked down by the backsplash of the passing wave or the feeling of sinking sand around your feet. There must be more, your heart cries. Where is the peace of God and the joy of the Lord that makes each day fresh and new and over-flowing with gratitude?

"Gideon replied, If God is with us, why has all this happened to us?"
Judges 6:13

This experience only comes through the reality of who you are to Christ. To "marry your maker" is the ceremony of all ceremonies. Years ago God gave me a vision I will never forget which transformed my life. It was a bride and groom's dance in the middle of an elaborate ballroom with shimmering floors. I was dressed in a pure white gown trimmed with lace, beads, and satin. I was held by the strong arms of my Savior, who was much taller than I. As we danced I leaned my head into his chest where I could hear his heartbeat and felt safety surround me. When I looked into His face His eyes stood out speaking such love and tenderness. But, what I envisioned next I wasn't prepared for. As He looked at me I had no body or face, just a beautiful white gown. What He said left me in tears of thanksgiving, "I do not see as the world sees. I see a beautiful bride spotless, whom I marry this day for what others don't see, her inward beauty." This may sound very simple to some, but at this point in my life it was this vision that changed my life and helped me realize who I really was to Christ. Not only did I see what He saw, I felt His tenderness and love greater than at any other time in my life. I will not forget the day I married my maker. My prayer is that all women experience this same feeling I felt in knowing how much I meant to my Savior.

Who are the women from Biblical days who discovered what it meant to marry their maker? There are numerous women who have played a significant role in helping us uncover our own feelings and find victory in similar situations. I want to break down these women in each of the five categories I mentioned this book is dedicated to. Our challenges are not always identical, yet we all must meet our challenges head on if we are going to be victorious. We must all discover what it means to marry our maker. (Many of these feelings I will talk about have been expressed to me by women who are in these situations today as well from my own heart.)

The Single Woman:

The greatest example I could possibly use for a single woman who knew what it meant to trust God in what was not a normal or for that matter accepted situation was Mary, the mother of Jesus.

Looking into her life we see she was a young single girl preparing for what was probably the moment she had dreamed of her whole life, true love. She was engaged to Joseph, but the fairy tale love story would take a great detour as God changed her direction. As any young girl does, Mary had probably had replayed that special day in her mind over and over. She had longed for Prince Charming to love her and desired to return his love. Consider for a minute Mary's thoughts as the angel of the Lord appeared to her and explained she would become pregnant through the work of the Holy Spirit. I can only imagine, she had many questions & thoughts:

What will Joseph think?
What will everyone say about me?
How can this turn out well?
My dream is fading from sight.
Will my family disown me?

We discover as Mary accepts the call of God in her life, complications do start to arise once she marries her maker and attaches herself to His call on her life. Obviously, Mary was quite afraid to tell Joseph what had happened. Maybe she thought that because they would soon be married and he would not question if the child was his? Maybe she was afraid he would no longer desire to be with her? We find that Joseph discovered her pregnancy. It was not through her news, but rather through the Holy Spirit. Joseph decided to divorce or dismiss her quietly so as to not draw attention to her situation. While he was trying to figure out how to go about this, an angel of God appeared to him and instructed him on what he was to do. Can you imagine the negativity that was attached to Mary as she continued to follow the plan God had made for her life? What was once a dream of the happily ever after changed courses for a bigger plan that would glorify God to a greater extreme. I would like to speak to the unwed mothers at this point. Although Mary was impregnated as a part of God's greater plan, the life that has been created in you has been planned for. The journey for the single, unwed mother is often scarred by choices that have cost her friendships, family relationships and condemnation by those she loves. Mary probably received some of the same condemnation and felt the loneliness you have felt at some point. Many have made the choice to carry their children to birth and promised to give these children the best they can despite the wishes of their mate to abort this precious life. Some women have fallen victim to the pressures of their companions to abort their unborn child or have made this choice themselves out of fear of inability to provide for the child. Whatever your circumstance the truth you must hold on to is this—regrets will never lead to restoration. The past cannot be changed, but the future can. Forgiveness must become a part of your life for yourself and for your child's father.

"He forgives your sins, every one."
Psalm 103:3

As a single woman, you may feel time is flying by and Prince Charming is nowhere to be found. For the single woman with child you may wonder if anyone will love you enough to accept the responsibility of a child who is not theirs. Let me promise you that God knows exactly what you need and He knows where it is. When you look to God and focus daily on His love He will work all things out for you.

"Steep your life in God-reality, God-initiative, God-provisions. Don't worry about missing out. You'll find all your everyday human concerns will be met. Give your entire attention to what God is doing right now and don't get worked up about what may or may not happen tomorrow. God will help you deal with whatever hard things come up when the time comes."

Matthew 6:33-34

This passage of scripture assures you that no matter what the challenge, whether it be loneliness for companionship or financial concerns God already has your back as you look to Him and Him alone.

The Married Woman:

This next story is of a woman who has an amazing strength and love that endures an extremely difficult marriage. Let me introduce you to Abigail. Abigail's story can be found in 1 Samuel 25. She was married to a very wealthy man. Her husband Nabal was a successful business man, obviously concerning himself with attaining more success. Not only was he wealthy, but evil and a drunkard. He lived for himself with no concern for the well-being of anyone else, including his family. King David had requested provisions of Nabal's hired hands. His servants told Nabal of David's request and his reply was, *"Who is this David? There are many servants this day, breaking away from their master."* His disregard of David's request placed him in an extremely dangerous situation. David set out to destroy him and his entire household for his denial of the request. One of the servants went to Abigail and told her of Nabal's denial and David's intent to destroy the household. It is important to note here that the servant told Abigail that no one could reason with Nabal because he was such a wicked man. Have you ever known anyone who is always right and cannot be reasoned with? Then you have met Nabal. Abigail intercepted the destruction by delivering provisions to King David in an attempt to protect her household. Later Abigail went to Nabal, but found him drunk so delayed telling him of her act until morning.

The Bible tells us Abigail was a very wise and beautiful woman. I can almost hear her heart crying out to God to change the heart of her husband, no doubt she did love him and wanted the best for him as well, hoping to be an important part of his life. She knew he could not be reasoned with and his drunken rages kept her from approaching him lest she place herself in a dangerous situation. It saddens me to say, many women today are married to Nabal. They fear speaking to their husband on any matters that might require something of him. They walk on eggshells watching what they say and when they say it. Something as simple as, "can you help me move the furniture or cook supper tonight?" can become a threat to the authority of her husband. He is in charge and not to be questioned, requested of or went around. In Abigail's case she showed wisdom in looking out for her household including her husband, however, she was wise to tell him of the events only after he sobered up. In doing so he fell dead as his heart stopped. I almost wonder if his frustration was not so much that King David was helped, but rather that his wife was the one he was

helped by and not Nabal himself. The following text, although not Nabal's response could very well have been. *"Why did you go out to fight...Without letting us go with you?...Jephthah said, "I did call you for help, but you ignored me. When I saw you weren't coming I took my life in my hands and confronted the Ammonites myself and God gave them to me!"*
Judges 12:1-2

A Nabal will almost always want to be the one calling the shots. In this case, he was asked to help but refused and Abigail stepped in to what God had willed for the situation in an effort to protect her family. We see this same mentality of control in the story of Jephthah. I also wonder if Nabal felt threatened by Abigail's independence and I can almost hear his words of condemnation toward her when she told him what she did believing it was God's will. Look at Jephthah's response to the men who opposed him below:

"So why did you show up here today? Are you spoiling for a fight with me?"
Judges 12:3

Many women today fear their husbands reactions to what seem like normal everyday conversations. They know that their actions, although sometimes favorable in the best interest of the family will result in a fight to rebuild the ego of their husband and a session of verbal attacks against them. They quickly learn they will be given what their spouse desires to give and when he desires to give it. Their desire to share what makes them feel loved is met with complaints of what she doesn't do to make him happy. She is expected to be happy with what she is given, to expect nothing in return and to always keep him upon a pedestal. She is meant to feel that she owes him. How did Abigail find the strength to stay with such a cruel man? Did Abigail know what she was walking into when she went to tell Nabal of her doings? I believe the strength of Abigail is found in her respect for the things of God. She knew King David was the Lord's chosen and this meant he should be respected. Abigail understood that what God put in place was to be honored and her reverence for God gave her the strength to face the consequences of a life lived for the things of

God despite her husband's expected reaction of disapproval. Her God-given secret of success is understanding the order of authority: God first, husband second. Unfortunately, many women are allowing bad marriages to wreck their lives instead of empower their lives. They often give up their purpose in pursuit of peace. Keep in mind, the purpose of your spouse has been compromised as well. That being said, to let your purpose die will not help your husband discover his. The greatest love you can show your spouse is a life sold out for the things of Christ, even if they look down upon this.

"There are husbands who, indifferent as they are to any words about God, will be captivated by your life of holy beauty."
1 Peter 3:1

If you are among the women who are married to a Nabal it is important to only speak what God instructs you to say.

"Say exactly what I tell you to say, Don't pull your punches..."
Jeremiah 1:17

When God gives you a message to deliver, remember it is He who is your fortress and place of safety. It may not go as you would hope, but the Holy Spirit will work it into the life of your husband. Remember the angel of the Lord's appearance to Joseph. His mind was not changed until the angel appeared to him. Mary could not change it.

"But, don't be afraid of them, son of man And don't be afraid of anything they say. Don't be afraid when living among them is like stepping on thorns or finding scorpions in your bed. Don't be afraid of their mean words or their hard looks….Your job is to speak to them. Whether they listen is not your concern…"
Ezekiel 2:4-7

I must say again, I am in no way advising a woman to stay with an abusive partner. It is only through God's guidance should this decision be made and I believe each woman must make this decision for herself. I will add that God does not look upon the abused woman who stays or leaves any differently. He loves his daughters and will always bottle their tears and comfort their hearts. He knows your pain, sees your pain and feels your pain and will always be the healer among the heartbroken no matter where your path leads. It is not God's will for any woman to be abused mentally, emotion ally, sexually economically or physically.

The Separated Woman:

Before I talk about this woman in the Bible. I want to talk about the heart of the separated woman in reference to to-day. The majority of separations are seen by couples who have children, especially young children. An estranged marriage is often only attempted for reconciliation for the sake of the children. However, in some cases one of the partners does not want a divorce and holds on to any hope in finding their path back to love with their mate. Separations often leave the woman (and man) dealing with further trust issues. However, in situations of abuse, this time apart can be a time for the couple to seek professional help in overcoming these strongholds. For many women this time can leave her feeling lonely, yet excited about gaining an independence that she has never been able to experience. It can also take a toll on her purpose and value. Many struggles can surface presenting questions like:

"Did I do all I could to be a good wife?"
"Did I tell my husband often enough how much I really love him?"
"Did I keep him satisfied sexually?"
"Was I the kind of mother he needed me to be to our children?"

As the independent newness of the separation begins to wear off, depression and loneliness can settle in placing her in a vulnerable state as men begin to show her attention. It is crucial during this time of separation that women invest in their spiritual well-being by seeking God more than they ever have. It is a time of learning who you are called to be and acting on that call. When your time is invested in moving forward in your purpose, it leaves less room for the enemy to take advantage of vacant time and greater chance for reconciliation.

"I am God, your God, who teaches you how to live right and well. I show you

what to do and where to go."
Isaiah 48:17

Be very careful at this point in life. You must take inventory of what you are hoping to gain from this separation which is usually a restored marriage with Christ at the center. A word of advice for the woman who finds herself in this transition as seen from the life of Joseph:

"The Lord was with Joseph and he pros-
pered and he lived in the house of his
Egyptian master....Potiphar's wife spoke to
Joseph day after day, but he did not listen
to her..."
Gen. 39:10

Notice Joseph was doing what God had called him to do, where he called him to do it, but this did not eliminate the temptation that was before him. However, Joseph held his ground and remained pleasing to God by not sacrificing his call for fleshly desires. During a separation women are often forced to find more stable employment often putting them into temptations they have not had to deal with to such extremes before. This does not mean they are not at the place God wants them to be, but rather at a cross roads of character building.

Now let's take a look at a woman in the Bible who separated herself from her husband. I want to look at the prostitute, Gomer. You may be wondering what could we possibly learn from Gomer? Through her life and of her husband, Hosea, we discover the love of God for His fallen people. Hosea married Gomer and had children by her per God's instructions. It was shortly thereafter that Gomer left Hosea (separated herself from him) and went back to her old way of living. What caused her to go back to her past? What strongholds kept her returning to a life of heartache and seduction? We do not know of Gomer's upbringing and what brought her to this place in life. Could she have been a sex slave from childhood? Was her mother a prostitute? We do not know. My heart grieves for the prostitute for her identity has been masked by what she can offer instead of who she really is. Her heart longs for love while she remains in bondage to mistruths about her value.

Many will eventually develop unconsciousness to their situation and began to see know other way to support themselves financially. These women need our help.

What we learn from Gomer's story is that God's love takes the brokenness of a woman (a prostitute) and shows her new value and acceptance. After Gomer left Hosea, he bought her back and loved her with a Godly love. (This story can be found in the book of Hosea.) I reference this story because for the separated woman she has had a husband and now often feels rejected and unloved. In her void she longs to be drawn back into the arms of her mate and be loved as God loves in tenderness and acceptance.

The Divorced Woman:

The road to recovery is extremely hard for the divorced woman. Up to this point she has shared her life and all of its aspects with a companion, raised the children with him, took family vacations, made memories and dreamed dreams. Financial obligations were once approached together and the security of knowing they could pull together in tough times always gave her a sense of safety. Now the burden of provision has fallen completely on her, the children's futures are often directed in two completely different paths and the memories have left a feeling of failure not easily overcome. As a woman faces the upcoming divorce her mind is flooded with fear for the children's well being, fear of finding someone to truly love her someday, fear of being alone, fear of financial struggle and the list goes on and on. She begins to question herself and may even ask herself, "Why can't anyone love me?," especially if she has had failed relationships in the past. This woman will often feel an inadequacy to be accepted again. Let's look at the Samaritan woman at the well.

"Jesus said,' Everyone who drinks the water I give will never thirst again.' The woman said, 'Sir give me this water so I won't ever get thirsty...' He said, 'Go and call your husband and then come back.' She said, 'I have no husband...' That's nicely put: I have no husband, but you have had five husbands and the man you

are living with is not your husband... 'It's who you are and the way you live that count before God. Your worship must engage your spirit in the pursuit of truth. That's the kind of people the Father is looking for: those who are simply and honestly themselves before him in their worship. "
John 4: 13-18,23-24

Jesus made it a point to talk to this woman. Not only was she a Samaritan, who Jews did not talk to, but she was a divorced woman. In her comments we can almost hear her telling Jesus that she is tired and thirsty for purpose and value. She feels the failure of five previous marriages, yet Jesus loves her enough to offer her purpose and commends her for her honesty. For someone to see something worthwhile in her life gave her new hope that things could be different. Maybe God had not forgotten about her and desired to change her life. This is seen when Jesus tells her this is the kind of person the Father is looking for. At this point she discovers hope and purpose for a life she had been routinely living with regret. Although she was still confused about the meaning of all this, she found herself in expectation of promise.

I have talked with many divorced women and heard over and over the difficulties they face with finding happiness. They can't seem to find enough purpose in their jobs, even though they may have very financially stable employment. They pour themselves into their children, but still have a longing for something more. For many who have left abusive relationships the peace they feel is a great relief and liberates them and their children to find a new sense of enjoyment in the simpler things in life. However, the natural desire for a companion creeps up as their outgoing love is greater than their incoming love. For the divorced woman the need to feel intimate with a companion is often strong since she has experienced this type of bonding before, even if the marriage was estranged. A woman once told me she felt especially vulnerable in his area and found herself uncomfortable around all men, afraid that she would allow her sexual desires to cause unwise decisions for a future mate. For the divorced woman she must encounter her maker at the well to find the living water which satisfies all areas of her life. At the appointed time God will cause her future mate to pursue her with love. I once heard a quote, "When you find someone chasing after God, keep up." Her focus directed on God will lead her to a fulfilled future.

"The steps of a good man are directed by the Lord..."
Psalm 37:23

The Widowed woman:

The emptiness felt by this woman cannot be replaced by reconciliation. Her life has taken a path that can't be changed leaving her with the challenge to continue living daily with the unanswered "why's." When this woman finds herself at this place she must hold tight to God and allow Him to cast away her fear. If you are this woman, casting away fear does not mean you don't question how you can go on, but rather that you know that God's ability is bigger than your doubt. At times when life seems to have the upper-hand remember, God has the

BIGGER hand & is always holding yours.

"My soul clings to You; Your right hand upholds me."
Psalm 63:8

I want to take you into the lives of two women in the Bible who had to overcome bitterness, tough decision making and financial challenge due to their widowhood. First, we turn our thoughts toward the widow at Zarephath. Her story can be found in 1 Kings 17. As she gathered sticks to cook one last meal--she continued to work till what appeared to be the end, for this was visibly the only meal she could prepare for herself and her son. Often the financial challenges and responsibility fall unexpectedly on the widowed woman? Her outlook could easily be one of discouragement, weariness and bitterness. But, we see from this widow a different story. She continued to cook as though she had food. She focused on what was at hand, not at what tomorrow would bring or not bring. Secondly, God had told her to provide for Elijah--she gave out of her need to remain God's servant. The wisdom of this widow is clearly seen. She understood all must be forsaken to serve God, even when it meant putting her child second, knowing God would bless her and lead her to provision for her child as she obeyed.

".....and he who loves [and takes more pleasure in] son or daughter more than [in] Me is not worthy of Me...He who does not take up his cross and follow Me [cleave steadfastly to Me, conforming wholly to My example in living and if need be, in dying also] is not worthy of Me....He who receives and welcomes and accepts a prophet because he is a prophet shall receive a prophet's reward..."
Matthew 10: 37-38, 41

The road of the widow can often be filled with difficult decisions requiring her to sacrifice her reasoning for God's purpose. Not all widows are those in their upper years. Many still have children to provide for. However, what the children learn through the actions of their mother will carry them through the difficult times of their lives. The widow at Zarephath viewed life honestly. She professed she was cooking her last meal. She was told by Elijah not to be afraid. The life of a widow can be plagued with fear because she knows she has no one she can fall back on. She often feels inferior to others believing they pity her in her present condition and does not want others to know of her needs.

"Fear not, for you will not be ashamed; be not confounded, for you will not be disgraced; for you will forget the shame of your youth, and the reproach of your widowhood you will remember no more. For your Maker is your husband, the Lord of hosts is his name; and the Holy One of Israel is your Redeemer, the God of the whole earth he is called.
Isaiah 54:4-5

Her maker is indeed her husband, her everything.

The second woman we want to look at is Naomi. Naomi's story is found in the first chapter of Ruth. Naomi found herself widowed and bereaved of two sons. This left her bitter towards the Lord.

"...it is far more bitter for me than for you

*that the hand of the Lord is gone out
against me....And when she arrived in
Bethlehem she said to them 'call me not
Naomi, (pleasant) call me Mara (bitter)
since the Lord has dealt very bitterly with
me. I went out full, but the Lord has
brought me home again empty. Why call
me Naomi, since the Lord has testified
against me, and the Almighty has afflicted
me?"
Ruth 1:13,19-21*

Not only was she bitter, but pitied her
condition and possibly doubted her husband's decision to have brought their family to the place where they were all taken
from her. The one thing we see in all the
"why's" of Naomi's situation is her devotion to her daughter-in-laws and the
guidance she gives them for a better life.
Her influence on Ruth changed Ruth's life.
The widow is not without purpose and her
acceptance to "marry her maker" and allow Him to lead her into the purpose for
her life is evident in Naomi's story.

Marrying your maker can mean different things to different women based
upon their individual needs. However, the

one thing it means to all women is that God can fill every void in her life and bring beautiful things from it.

Do you ever feel like you are just hanging in there. You may even feel like a professional hanger. God says in *2 Timothy 1:13-14, "Keep at your work, faith and love rooted in Christ, guard this precious gift given unto you."* In other words, "Keep doing what you are called to do through HIS faith, love and strength. Guard your calling and don't quit hanging. Hangers are clothed with beautiful things! May God clothe you today with beautiful blessings as you depend upon HIS strength, love and faith to carry you through!

"There has never been the slightest doubt in my mind that the God who started this great work in you would keep at it and bring it to a flourishing finish…."
Philippians 1:6

Marry your maker today and He will never leave you nor forsake you no matter what life brings your way. You don't make it through your circumstance because you are strong or wise. You make it through because you are loved and have a God who marries you, for better or worse, richer or poorer, in sickness and in health, never parting not even in the end of your journey. Your confidence and security are in the one who has given you life. It is not your circumstance that defines your value or your provision, but your maker.

"Look at the birds! They don't worry about what to eat—they don't need to sow or reap or store up food—for your heavenly Father feeds them. And you are far more valuable to him than they are....And if God cares so wonderfully for flowers that are here today and gone tomorrow, won't he more surely care for you, O men of little faith? " Matthew 6:28,30

Chapter 4

A Double Portion

"Strength for the Battle of the Body"

The emotional and mental struggles a woman faces will almost always affect her physical well-being in some way or another. In chapter 1 I discussed how stress can take a huge toll on the physical body through exhaustion and disease. As a woman approaches middle age those challenges can often be escalated as stress plays a huge role on her hormonal balance. The effects can be anything from hot flashes to temporary memory loss. I experienced this first hand. Finding myself driving down the interstate one day. I became completely unable to determine my location. Knowing this was not even close to normal, I called my doctor and set up an appointment. What she found was that my hormone levels were completely out of balance and determined it was due to a very stressful situation I was currently in the middle of. Fortunately, I was able to get on a prescription for bio-identical hormones and alleviate these symptoms.

In this chapter I want to talk about how the emotional and mental struggles we often encounter as women can be detrimental to our physical well-being as well as the physical abuse a woman often encounters.

Years ago when I struggled with anorexia and bulimia many who were close to me could not understand why these illnesses had such a grip on me. They did not see what I saw and therefore expected me to see with their eyes and stop this behavior. Often what you cannot see becomes the hardest for you to believe.

"Blessed are they that have not seen and yet have believed."
John 20:29

Although this is one of the most difficult things to do, you must take God at His word and look through His eyes. In the song "Fingerprints of God" by Steven Curtis Chapman the lyrics say, "I can see the tears falling from your eyes, I know where they're coming from, a heart broken into by what you don't see, the person in the mirror doesn't look like a magazine, I know you're a masterpiece creation quietly applauds covered with the fingerprints of God." Many women's hearts are broken as they shed tears in mirrors. In her eyes her beauty may only go skin deep or may seem hidden only below the surface. Some see flaws no one else sees, while others have their flaws pointed out to them by their companion. This hurt is a devastation that runs deep and is not easily recovered from. Some women suffer from verbal attacks regarding their weight, sex drive, hair, dress attire, beauty etc…. I know women whose spouses will admire the beauty of petite women, while mocking and disgusting over heavier women, belittling their spouse's size. This rejection will crush the heart of a woman and leave her feeling unworthy and unloved. Much in the same way, a spouse's struggle with pornography outwardly rejects his wife by suggesting she is not enough for him to be satisfied with. Let's take this a little farther to the wife in the bedroom. The greatest gift God gave us is love. Love is made complete when a couple can share one another in intimacy of appreciation for the spouse God has given them. Although for men, this drive is more physically focused, a woman usually is more drawn by the emotional force that exists between her and her spouse. If that emotional need to feel loved is not met and she becomes an object to be obtained ,her sexual satisfaction remains unmet. For many women they become what I referred to at the beginning of the book—the prostitute behind closed doors of a marriage. When a woman's sole purpose is keeping her husband's needs met, with disregard to her own, loneliness, rejection, and depression set in quickly. Because of the importance of this physical bond between husband and wife and the emotional ties it is supposed to bring to the surface it can become a form of payment rather than uniting in the relationship when it is one sided. She will often be told untrue statements like:

"You must not love me, you don't show it."

"Do whatever you women who don't like to have sex do."

"You don't touch me enough"

"Why do I have to earn it by rubbing your back?"

"If you won't have sex I won't pay the bills?"

Many women find themselves almost totally without quality communication until it comes time for bed. Her response to the request is expected to be passion and initiation even when she feels rejected inwardly. Her beauty becomes surface satisfaction. Many times she will be expected to behave as a prostitute further damaging her self-esteem and bringing a tremendous amount of guilt and shame. This same woman will often be reprimanded if she has not made sure her husband is well taken care of before she starts her monthly cycle. She is often reminded of all he does for her and she should respond at his will because it is her scriptural duty. Women, you are not to be treated as objects or puppets, but treasures, especially by your spouses. Sex without love is not God's plan for intimacy in a marriage. Sexual complaints aimed at your partner are the most damaging and will tear down a woman's value in a heartbeat. In most cases it is not that a woman does not desire her spouse or have a need for sex, but rather feels no significance to him as a person and cannot surface physical passion without emotional attachment. Unfortunately, this leaves many women as prisoners in their minds. They become prostitutes in their minds to fulfill the desires of their spouse for this is the only way they reach sexual satisfaction and assure him he is doing a good job. This often leaves her dreading the night and the expectations put upon her. Although this may appear to be a negative view of a husband's behavior, it is not meant to condemn, but only to reveal the truth of what many women experience every day. Many feel alone and singled out as a misfit, wondering if there really is something wrong with them. Only in surfacing these emotions can a woman begin the healing process and change her self-image. Sorrow may endure for a night, but joy cometh in the morning. The heartaches of today can be lessened by the hopes of tomorrow. For although we may not know what tomorrow holds, we do know who holds tomorrow. What looks like devastation to us is God's opportunity to work a miracle. A broken heart & unraveling life can be healed & empowered as we call out for God's help. The strength rises that is not yours or anyone else's, but God's alone.

"Heal the breaks! Everything is coming apart at the seams...Give us help for the hard task; human help is worthless. In

God we'll do our very best; he'll flatten
the opposition for good."
Psalm 60:2,11-12

God will heal the hurting woman even when her life seems to be without hope. When we do our best, God does the rest. But, how can I love when the hurt runs so deep, you may ask? The power to love is enabled through the Spirit not the flesh. When we understand that we can love the one who has hurt us without loving the hurt we begin to heal and receive adequate spiritual love even when fleshly love is almost nonexistent.

"A new commandment I give to you, that you love one another: just as I have loved you, you also are to love one another. "
John 13:34

Another area where women often face physical persecution is during illness. I knew someone who dealt daily with emotional, economic and sexual abuse. Her life was kept in tears by the hurtful put downs, name calling, humiliation, destruction, obsession with money and angry behavior. She developed cancer after many years of marriage. One would naturally think this would serve as a wake-up call to the abusive spouse causing him to fear losing his companion. However, this was not the case and she suffered much persecution. The sad part of this story is that it wasn't until after her death that he realized how much he had lost. Although this might seem discouraging, it will hopefully serve as a wake-up call to any men who might read this book and for women to understand her love of the Lord will be her strength daily. Often the hardest challenges for women are those in direct contempt against her physical well-being spoken through unconcern for her suffering.

Another area especially hard to look at is that of physical abuse. Often denial of the intensity of the abuse leaves women believing statements like:

"It's not as bad as what it could have been"
"Maybe if I wouldn't have responded the way I did, I wouldn't have been hurt."
"Maybe I deserved it"
"I don't want to hurt them by telling about it."

"My dear daughter...broken, shattered, and yet they put on band-aids, saying, 'It's not so bad..you'll be just fine'..but things are not 'just fine.'
Jeremiah 8:10-12

Abuse is wrong in any form and physical abuse is not only emotionally damaging, but dangerous. For if a man cannot control his anger and must express it through contact, he is not in control of the extensiveness or the outcome. God takes these things very seriously.

"Now the works of the flesh are evident: sexual immorality, impurity, sensuality, idolatry, sorcery, enmity, strife, jealousy, fits of anger, rivalries, dissensions, divisions, envy, drunkenness, orgies, and things like these....as I warned you before, that those who do such things will not inherit the kingdom of God."
Galatians 5:19-21

"He who dwells in the shelter of the Most High will abide in the shadow of the Almighty. I will say to the Lord, "My refuge and my fortress, my God, in whom I trust." For he will deliver you from the

snare of the fowler and deadly pestilence. He will cover you... under his wings you will find refuge; his faithfulness is a shield and buckler. You will not fear the terror of the night, nor the arrow that flies by day,"
Psalm 91:1-16

It is crucial that a woman in this position hold tight to her Lord, seeking, listening and acting upon His direction and finding her place of safety. If you find yourself suffering under physical persecution, my prayer for you is that God will grant you a double portion of strength and above all of His spirit directing decisions to be made. For to be led by His Spirit is to enter rest and safety. God is a righteous judge and avenges the broken and mistreated giving strength to the weary.

"...And Elisha said, 'I pray you, let a double portion of your spirit be upon me."
2 Kings 2:9

"Because you got a double dose of trouble and more than your share of contempt, Your inheritance in the land will be doubled and your joy go on forever."
Isaiah 61:7

Chapter 5

Removing the Camouflage

"Behind Enemy Lines-
Knowing Your Foe"

It is so easy to blame those who cause us pain, claiming that their actions become our reactions. However, we each have the ability to control our own behavior and how we react to situations. It is important that we take a closer look at what and who lies below the surface of all actions in order to understand what is going on. God is truth and Satan is a liar. Satan will seek to penetrate the lives of God's children keeping them bound by greed, lust and all other forms and behaviors of sinfulness. He does not play favorites, he desires to mislead and destroy the future of all mankind. If you do not know your enemy and his tactics it is impossible to know how to fight or what position to take. In war the soldier must be prepared, he must know his enemy's weaknesses, strengths, plan of attack and whereabouts at all times. It is no different for the woman on the battlefield. Her best defense is preparation and position with Christ.

Whoever makes a practice of sinning is of the devil, for the devil has been sinning from the beginning. The reason the Son of God appeared was to destroy the works

of the devil. "
1 John 3:8

"He was a murderer from the beginning, and has nothing to do with the truth, because there is no truth in him. When he lies, he speaks out of his own character, for he is a liar and the father of lies. "
John 8:44

Understand this—anything that sets itself up against the word of God is a lie. If condemnation is ever present in your life, it is not of God, but of Satan. In other words, if you are not being admonished as a means of wanting the best for you, the deliverer of the word is not being led by God, but by his or her own selfish desires.

"Let no foul or polluting language, nor evil word nor unwholesome or worthless talk [ever] come out of your mouth, but only such [speech] as is good and beneficial to the spiritual progress of others, as is fitting to the need and the occasion, that it may be a blessing and give grace (God's favor) to those who hear it."
Ephesians 4:29

Yes, you can determine if the words spoken to you are from God or if they are being controlled by Satan, thus attacking you position of confidence.

"Brethren, if any person is overtaken in misconduct or sin of any sort, you who are spiritual [who are responsive to and controlled by the Spirit] should set him right and restore and reinstate him, without any sense of superiority and with all gentleness, keeping an attentive eye on yourself, lest you should be tempted also."
Galatians 6:1

Notice, gentleness and restoration will be the heart of one controlled by the Spirit not superiority. Now we understand that many of the relationships we have with companions and the world in general are often contaminated with Satan's agenda and not God's purpose. Satan's agenda is to destroy you. God's agenda is to fulfill His purpose in your life.

"Be sober-minded; be watchful. Your adversary the devil prowls around like a roaring lion, seeking someone to devour."

1 Peter 5:8

"The thief comes only to steal and kill and destroy. I came that they may have life and have it abundantly."
John 10:10

"But I am afraid that as the serpent deceived Eve by his cunning, your thoughts will be led astray from a sincere and pure devotion to Christ. "
2 Cor. 11:3

"And no wonder, for even Satan disguises himself as an angel of light. "
2 Cor. 11:14

Satan is sly and will not usually make a grand entrance. He will slowly lead a person astray through their thinking, pulling them farther from God. It is often difficult for those under Satan's control to see what is going on. Satan moves subtlety with small steps of wrong thinking eventually defiling a person's conscience.

"The Spirit makes it clear that as time goes on, some are going to give up on the faith and chase after demonic illusions

put forth by professional liars. These liars have lied so well and for so long that they've lost their capacity for truth. "
1 Timothy 4:1-2

One of the saddest things about the bondage of the abuser is that they are unaware to the enemy's attack and before they know it, everything they have has disappeared. Wives become emotionally detached, children become distanced, friendships become nonexistent, and job relationships become strained and the one controlled by the enemy is left alone, disheartened, angry, depressed and unaware of what has happened and often looks for someone to blame for their unhappiness.

"[Jesus] saw the city and wept over it, saying, 'If you had known... especially in this your day, the things that make for your peace! But now they are hidden from your eyes. For days will come upon you when your enemies will build an embankment around you, surround you and close you in on every side, and level you, and your children within you, to the ground; and they will not leave in you one stone upon another, because you did not

know the time of your visitation."
Luke 19:41-44

I must add a note in here regarding the power of Satan in the mind of the woman. She often inflicts herself with condemnation, trying so hard to be worthy of God's purpose in her life that she creates roadblocks to the Promised Land. The fact is, we are not worthy, but chosen, not perfect, but forgiven through the free gift of God's grace. We are too busy trying to earn it that we miss it. Let me ask you, "Do you know who is controlling your destiny when you do this?" Is not condemnation the very presence of Satan surfacing through your mind to hold you in defeat? A woman who is codependent will often allow this because she knows her weaknesses and sinfulness. She is misusing humility in its purpose which is to produce a heart of thanksgiving for God not produce bondage for who she isn't. This leaves her beaten down, beaten up, broken and beyond expectation of God's goodness to her. She must be set free from this condemnation by accepting the goodness of God and rejecting the perfection of self. The pressure she places on herself to obtain perfection must be surrendered to Christ's acceptance of her through what was completed on the cross. For this is when she is triumphant over sin.

"For the sin of this one man, Adam, caused death to rule over many. But even greater is God's wonderful grace and his gift of righteousness, for all who receive it will live in triumph over sin and death through this one man, Jesus Christ."
Romans 5:17

Finally, unmasking who your enemy is will allow you to look beyond your faults and the faults of others and see the truth of who is behind the battle. For the suffering of the abuser is as great as for the one who suffers the abuse. The abused can have inner peace in outer conflict and live a life of joy amongst their sufferings, unlike the torment of the abuser who remains in constant inner turmoil. Stop living in defeat and allowing others to determine your worth. Know your God, know your foe and position yourself with God's word for strength.

Chapter 6

A Thorn In The Flesh

"Becoming Better Not Bitter"

One of the hardest questions to answer always seems to be, "How do I know what is God's will for my life in this situation?" Many women who struggle with insecurity arisen from verbal condemnation will often find it hard to determine what the truth is. They have often been put down for so long by others, they have begun to doubt their ability to discern anything, even God's plan for their life. As I've already discussed, this places them even more apt to become codependent on their companion, listening to everything he says, whether good or bad. Even for those women who are awakened to the truth for their life, they struggle to forgive their abuser and themselves. When it comes to forgiving, it is mandatory for a woman to separate the truth from a lie.

So how can a woman whose eyes have been opened break free from anger, frustration and fear of ever trusting others again. The answer lies in trusting her God to manifest His goodness through her life. Ultimate freedom comes when a woman can uncover the truth and trust her Savior. When she learns to trust God with everything including her finances, feelings and future, she no longer puts the pressure of perfection on others or on herself. Let me explain what I mean. A woman who has been let down in past relationships will struggle to trust future potential companions. She will often either put up a wall and reject love or put up her expectations and demand love. Both of these mentalities will imprison her to unhappiness. It is only when she is able to trust God with her companion's life that she can walk in freedom knowing God has it covered. When she rejects love, she walks away from ever being complete. When she demands love, she puts the pressure of perfection on those she loves. Man will always make mistakes and come up short, but God never fails and can always be depended upon even when it comes to caring for her mate.

It is often hard to forgive and love those who hurt you with no purpose other than to advance their own wishes. When we can look beyond the eyes of the attacker and the words of the belittler we can begin to see the pain of the abuser. God's heart weeps for those held captive in any sense. He loves the sinner and desires to set them free from Satan's control. Their lives are in turmoil from past abuse, present situations and future fears opening them up to bitterness toward God. When a man's heart is bitter toward his maker, nothing in his life will be at peace, including his relationships with others. The abuser will often be angry with God over promises that are not yet manifested or feel abandoned by God in their own life.

Although the pain runs deep for those who are the abuser's constant attempt to regain control of his own life, love must be rooted in the one being abused. How can I love this person who tears me down, harms me and hates me you may be asking? With Christ's love is my answer. If you are full of God's love and know His compassion for the sinner, you can overcome your hate and love with Christ's love. Although human love seems limited, God's love never lacks.

..."and may you be able to feel and understand, as all God's children should, how long, how wide, how deep, and how high his love really is; and to experience this

love for yourselves, though it is so great that you will never see the end of it or fully know or understand it. And so at last you will be filled up with God himself. "
Ephesians 3:19

Human love cannot surpass the pain of abuse, but when you are filled with God himself and know the depths of His love you can do all things, including loving the abuser and weeping for their inner suffering.

"I can do all things through Christ who strengthens me."
Philippians 4:13

When her God-given ability to love surpasses her own ability, she will find herself inwardly grieving for the one who has hurt her. When we can look beyond the eyes of the attacker and the words of the belittler we can begin to see the pain of the abuser.

"Be happy with those who are happy, and weep with those who weep."
Romans 12:15

She begins to desperately long for his happiness and pray for his ability to find it. But, her sacrifice cannot be a life of complacency, giving up her purpose to meet his demands. This will never satisfy the person she longs to please (in any type of relationship) only shift the control to keep her codependent in another area of her life. She will always find herself coming up short in bringing this person happiness. Because women have a strong tie to their families first, they often feel they cannot effectively accomplish purpose outside the home if they cannot accomplish it within the home. However, they must remember, man has a free will and they cannot control what others do or how they respond. With this inability to control their home life, their purpose as a wife or companion will inwardly meet with a sense of failure, thus keeping them outwardly captive from moving into their purpose. This is a woman's thorn in the flesh. This dissatisfaction eats away at her life, knowing she was called to more, but remaining complacent. The thorn digs deep burying itself below several layers of pain, suffering and fear. Her complacency, codependency and insecurity have now become her world. It is often hard for a woman to determine where the thorn has entered, but once it is there it begins to produce continuous pain. It will often be invisible to the outside world for she hides it well in her attempts to be strong and endure the pain she is feeling. When the pain becomes too much it can fester and bring to the surface feelings of bitterness. If it is left to remain buried, it will almost always infect her body with daily inner suffering. The decision to dig out the thorn will be the hardest task for a woman, because it requires her to face her pain and step up to her purpose. It is not always met with praise. The discovery of her purpose can often become a thorn in the flesh of her companion or even co-workers. Their desire to feel needed or important may seem threatened by her desire to fulfill her purpose. It is at this crossroads that women decide to walk into their faith, step up to their purpose, and experience their healing or remain bound by the thorn that places limitations on their lives. A woman's ultimate desire is that of others to support her new found health and love her more each day, shar-ing in her victory. Unfortunately, this does not always happen and she must make the hard choice of walking the path alone. A woman who finds her purpose can forgive herself and others and leave her past as she embraces her future, even when it means leaving behind what she values most.

"You are blessed when you feel you've lost what is most dear to you. Only then can you be embraced by the One most dear to you."
Matthew 5:4

"The Lord will not allow the [uncompromisingly] righteous to famish, but He thwarts the desire of the wicked. "
Proverbs 10:3

God has his hand on the pure of heart and will not allow them to suffer beyond which they are capable of enduring. There is an end to the battle and a victory ahead for the woman who loves beyond her pain.

"Keep a cool head. Stay alert. The Devil is poised to pounce, and would like nothing better than to catch you napping. Keep

your guard up. You're not the only ones plunged into these hard times. It's the same with Christians all over the world. So keep a firm grip on the faith. The suffering won't last forever. It won't be long before this generous God who has great plans for us in Christ—eternal and glorious plans they are!—will have you put together and on your feet for good. He gets the last word; yes, he does. "
1 Peter 5:9-10

Bitterness left in place will steal the future of the woman of God. To remain bitter is to be void of joy and to wander in confusion. If we desire to be set free and to live a life of purpose, we must let go of all bitterness.

"Let all bitterness and wrath and anger and clamor and slander be put away from you, along with all malice. Be kind to one another, tenderhearted, forgiving one another, as God in Christ forgave you "
Ephesians 4:31-32

We are commissioned to be kind, even when the kindness is not returned. We can love the sinner and hate the sin.

"You have heard that it was said, 'You shall love your neighbor and hate your enemy.' But I say to you, Love your enemies and pray for those who persecute you,
Matthew 5:43-44

To travel the road of purpose we must break up the ground of bitterness repaving it with betterness. This is not an easy road and it is walked one day at a time, one step at a time, one thought at a time. Take each hurt under submission replacing it with the love of Christ which will overpower your pain and temptation to become bitter.

"I'm not saying I have this all together, that I have made it. But I am well on my way, reaching out for Christ, who has so wondrously reached out for me....By no means do I count myself an expert in all of this, but I've got my eye on the goal, where God is beckoning us onward—to Jesus. I'm off and running and I'm not turning back. So let's keep focused on that goal, those of us who want everything God has for us."

Philippians 3:12-15

Chapter 7

The Closer I Got The Farther I Fell

"When Serving God Brings Persecution"

Have you ever noticed it often seems the more you do right, the harder it is to gain ground? If so, you are not alone. You see, the enemy has a plan for your failure. His desire is to keep you as far away from discovering God's plan for your life as possible. I would almost venture to say, this is his number one goal against all people. If he can accomplish this task then you will not change the world for Christ and be His witnesses. It is impossible for the sick to help the sick. On the other side of the coin, we see that if we, through the Holy Spirit's revelation, discover who we are and what we are called to do, then the battle is won and lives will be changed for the glory of God. I promise you this is the last thing Satan wants and he will do all he can to distract you from discovering the plan God has for your life. He will distract you by busyness through unexpected events or delays. If this does not work, he will attempt to wear you out through lack of sleep, exhaustion and lack of concentration. The hardest attack he uses is often the one inflicted upon you by those you love through harsh words, unkindness and often threats of abandonment to pressure you into fear and action to guard your future. If he can change your focus he will be able to change your direction, thus keeping you away from your confidence in Christ. Fear still remains the number one tactic used to stop people from experiencing victory. We have all heard the saying, "Fear, is false evidence appearing real." Satan is a master of providing false evidence that is easily mistaken as truth.

"Look the land over, see what it's like, assess the people: Are they strong or weak? Are they few or many? Observe the land: Is it harsh or pleasant? Describe the towns where they live: Are they open camps or fortified within walls. And the soil: Is it fertile or barren? Are there forests?....The only thing is; the people who live there are fierce...."
Numbers 13:17-20, 28

We must learn to identify the tactics of Satan. Examine the character of those opposing you. Examine their interactions with others. What type of fruit is their life producing? This is not to judge them, but rather to understand the threat they pose in leading you off course of what we are called to do. Once you can understand what Satan is using to defeat you time and time again you can finally, once and for all, put a stop to it.

"Let's go up and take the land—now. We can do it."
Numbers 13:30

A woman will always face a cross-road of decision in life. See the diagram below:

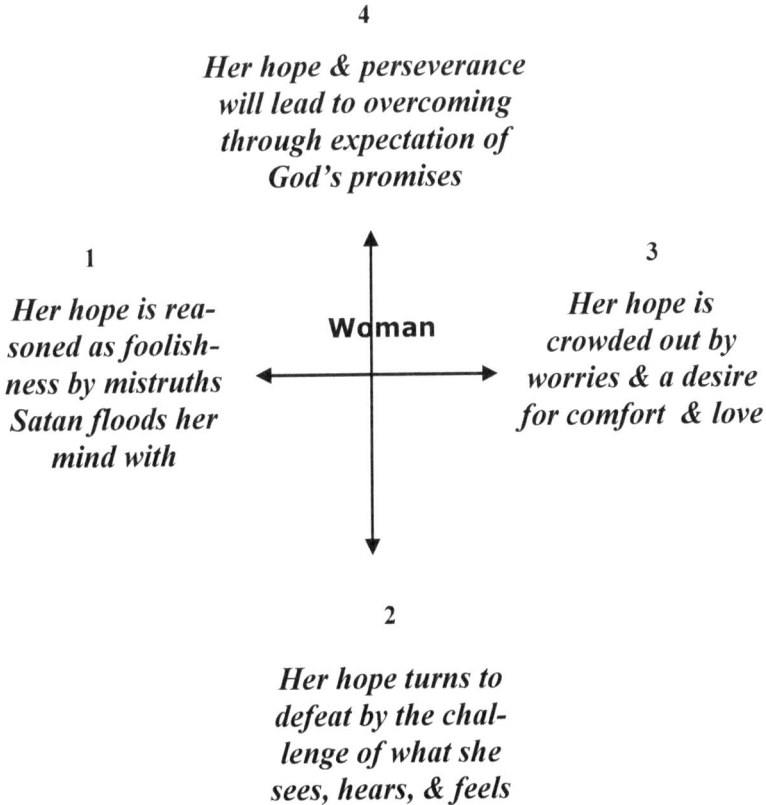

4

Her hope & perseverance will lead to overcoming through expectation of God's promises

1

Her hope is reasoned as foolishness by mistruths Satan floods her mind with

Woman

3

Her hope is crowded out by worries & a desire for comfort & love

2

Her hope turns to defeat by the challenge of what she sees, hears, & feels

"The farmer plants the word. Some people are like the seed that falls on the hardened soil of the road. No sooner do they hear the Word than Satan snatches away what has been planted in them. (diag. box 1) And some are like the seed that lands in the gravel. When they first hear the word, they respond with great enthusiasm. But there is such shallow soil of character that when the emotions wear off and some difficulty arrives, there is nothing to show for it. (diag. box 2) The seed cast in the weeds represents the ones who hear the kingdom news but are overwhelmed with worries about all the things they have to do and all the things they want to get. The stress strangles what they heard, and nothing comes of it. (diag. box 3) But the seed planted in the good earth represents those who hear the word, embrace it and produce a harvest beyond their wildest dreams." (diag. box 4) Mark 4:14-20

We can clearly see what the enemy is using to try and destroy us in this chart, however, we have the power to overcome the persecution. As women, we must test all things that so easily come against our minds and line them up with what the word of God says about us. It is His word spoken to us which is truth, not the condemning words of man. Let me note another avenue Satan will often take to convince you of your insignificance. Often times he may use someone to point out a scripture from God's word to convince you of your failures pointing out that you are not living according to God's word. They will do this in attempt to say, "God is saying to you…." It is very important scripture be taken in its entirety not picking and choosing what brings about the desired outcome. There are times, however, when God uses others to help you back on the path through His word, however it will always be done in love for the betterment of the individual not for the purpose of the message deliverer's comfort and desires. This is why Christ tells us,

"Don't suppress the Spirit, and don't stifle those who have a word from the Master. On the other hand, don't be gullible. Check out everything and keep only what's good. Throw out anything tainted with evil."
1 Thessalonians 5:19-22

In this life we will have persecution, especially when we are on the path to self-discovery through Christ. But Christ has promised us,

"Beloved, do not be surprised at the fiery trial when it comes upon you to test you, as though something strange were happening to you. But rejoice insofar as you share Christ's sufferings, that you may also rejoice and be glad when his glory is revealed. If you are insulted for the name of Christ, you are blessed, because the Spirit of glory and of God rests upon you."
1 Peter 4:12-14

To know that we walk hand in hand with God and that His glory is being manifested through our lives empowers us on to victory, peace and happiness.

The call on your life does not come without cost. Many times the cost is the lack of support or denial of by family and friends who know you. Could it be that they see your shortcomings or judge you unworthy or could it be they desire to be where you are and feel rejected? Be encouraged! A call is not placed on the perfect but rather on those who are willing to answer it. Jesus used the imperfect to reach the world. We are all imperfect, but made perfect in Christ as we submit to Him.

"Is this not the carpenter....And they took offense at Him and were hurt (that is they disapproved of him and it hindered them from acknowledging his authority) and they were caused to stumble and fall."
Mark 6:3

"Jesus said, a prophet is not without honor EXCEPT in his own country and among his own relatives and in his own house. And he was not able to do even one work of power there..."
Mark 6:4-5

"And he marveled because of their unbelief AND he went about among the surrounding nations AND CONTINUED TEACHING."
Mark 6:6

Do not allow the discouragement or condemnation from others keep you from doing what you know you're called to do.

Move forward and move on and let God deal with the discourager. Their judgment is not an indicator of your ability.

Hardship should be endured as a stepping stone not embraced as a tombstone. When we endure with eyes of a fulfilled & complete life we put to death eyes of defeat. How are you viewing your circumstances today?

"Those who keep their heads on straight will teach crowds right from wrong by their example. They'll be put to severe testing FOR A SEASON....the testing will refine, cleanse and purify those who keep their heads on straight and stay true, for there is still more to come.....men and women who live wisely and well will shine brilliantly...and those who put others on the right path will glow like stars forever."
Daniel 11:33-35, 12:3

We must choose to be a star for Christ in a world of conflict!

Peace is something we all desire, but is not always easily obtained. Do not confuse peace with passiveness. Peace is not found in passiveness, but often through persecution. The temptation to be passive by pleasing others in order to retain peace is not the goal God wants us to focus on. We are to do all we can to obtain peace without changing the direction God has asked us to go.

"There are many out there taking other paths, choosing other goals, and trying to get you to go along with them. I've warned you of them many times; sadly I'm having to do it again. All they want is easy street....but easy street is a dead end street." Phillippians 3:18

To focus on self-comfort is to take your eyes off Christ which will lead you down a dead end road. Know what God's called you to do (it will bring peace to your spirit) and stop letting others steal your peace by trying to change your focus from Christ to them. This will only keep us wandering in the wilderness like the Israelites and unfortunately will not be a testimony to them of God's faithfulness. If we choose to be an enabler to others, surrendering God's call on our life to keep peace then we choose to hurt those we love and want to help the most.

Who is this woman of God? Can she really exist and rise above the challenges of codependency, insecurity and depression? It is you! Yes, she does exist and she is in the mirror every day, reflecting the beauty that God sees.

"She tastes & sees (discerns, is aware of) that her gain from work (the blessings bestowed on her through the efforts she puts forth in her calling)with & for God (doing the work for God, with his help & to bring him glory)is good. Her lamp (the truth she knows that exposes evil) goes not out, but it burns on continually through the night (she rises at night to intercede for her family) of trouble (difficulty, distress, anxiety) privation (depriving of food, money & rights), or sorrow (great unhappiness, disappointment or wrong done), WARNING away fear (of provision, of loneliness, abuse), doubt (uncertainty of the future, lack of confidence in who she is), distrust (unsurety of God's intervention, vain imaginations)"

Proverbs 31:18

You are the woman who sees and identifies the blessings of God and quickly awakens to the enemy's plans to destroy these blessings. Rising at night to guard your family with prayer & spoken belief in an all-powerful God, you are aware of the enemy's plans to bring pain, anxiety, and sorrow through heartbreak, distress and depriving you of the necessities of life (food, money, and what is rightfully yours --respect, love & tenderness). You destroy & run off fear (knowing you are not given the spirit of fear, but rather of power, love & a strong mind—though you walk through the shadow of death, you fear no evil for God is with you—you fear not he who can kill the body, for he cannot kill the soul). You cast off doubt in your ability to fulfill the call on your life (for you know that in doubt you become like a wave of the sea, tossed to and fro unable to hold ground). You rebuke distrust (for you know to trust God with all your heart and not lean on your own understanding.) You are dependent on God for strength, when you are weary in body from the night watch. You know that you can do

ALL things through Christ who strengthens you--for God's presence goes with you and He will give you rest--for you know the fear of The Lord leads to life & you can rest content from trouble)

To God belongs all glory for equipping the woman of God to persevere through the persecution till she tastes the victory!

"You're blessed when your commitment to God provokes persecution. The persecution drives you even deeper into God's kingdom, not only that—count yourselves blessed every time people put you down or throw you out or speak lies about you to discredit me. What it means is that the truth is too close for comfort. You can be glad when that happens—give a cheer, even! For thought they don't like it, I do. And all heaven applauds. And know that you are in god company. My prophets and witnesses have always gotten into this kind of trouble."
Matthew 5:10-12

"For I know the plans I have for you, declares the Lord, plans to prosper you and

*not to harm you, plans to give you hope
and a future."*

Jeremiah 29:11

You are blessed woman of God and victorious over the persecution of the enemy. Declare it in forward faith and walk out your destiny!

Chapter 8

Sweet Surrender

"When Tears & Fears Meet Wisdom"

One thing the insecure woman does not believe she has is wisdom. She often feels her choices must somehow be confirmed by others to make them right. This insecurity attracts those who will often, even though they mean well, try and excessively advise her about even the simplest daily decisions. They will often overly look out for her making her feel even more inadequate. In regard to a controlling companion, he may always question and often degrade her decisions, especially about her dreams, business ventures and the children with no Biblical proof to back up his words. This very behavior can leave her imprisoned in her mind, her business and her home. When this happens she can no longer walk in confidence toward her purpose, but finds herself walking in the shadows of someone she has become codependent on. For this woman, trying to gain independence is a battle. She takes a step out of the shadow only to have someone make a suggestion in something she is doing and she immediately feels rejected and falls back into the shadows. Although, the suggestion was in no way directed at her as an attack, because of past abuse she views it as such. For many women in hurting and abusive relationships where this insecurity is present, her fear of being able to have enough wisdom to care for her children or live on her own become her prison. This is where her tears and fears run wild and keep her from believing she was created equal with as much purpose as everyone else.

In the shadows she has made her home and isolated herself from her independent purpose. Years of isolation and insecurity lead to an incapacitating bondage that is difficult to break free from and understand. The heart of loneliness settles in and can put her into emotional captivity stealing her life's potential friendships, opportunities, future love and above all happiness. In her occasional steps out of the shadows she faces responses like:

"How can you neglect your children?"
"Don't you care about me?"
"You are so stuck on yourself."
"You just live for yourself and your pleasure."
"God won't bless you."

This attempt to keep her isolated will either become her prison or her freedom depending on how she responds to it. Often in an effort to keep peace she will walk on eggshells to meet the wishes of the commenter as opposed to being true to her heart and purpose and denying these comments the power to control her choices.

"If it is possible, as far as it depends on you, live at peace with everyone."*
Romans 12:18

To this I must say it is not always possible to live at peace. Love and kindness should be your response, not denial of your purpose. God must be first! When you are being held captive and told to neglect what you believe are the dreams and purposes God has given you, you must make the decision to follow God even when it means turmoil instead of peace. When Jesus went into the temple and drove out the money changers he said:

"...My house shall be called a house of prayer; but you have mad it a den of robbers."

Matthew 21:13

Are we not the temple of Christ?

"Do you not know that your body is the temple of the Holy Spirit who lives within you....you are not your own?"
1 Cor. 6:19

If we do not belong to ourselves, but to Christ, should we not be fulfilling His purpose for our lives and not others purposes for us? Have we allowed our temple to be robbed of our purpose and value? Ladies, it is God's will that we walk out of the shadows and into the footsteps of Christ.

Let me go back to my earlier comments concerning isolation and the restrictions keeping us in it through denial of outside friendships. For the woman who has heard the comments pointing her toward selfishness, guilt will often follow in regards to her family and responsibilities. She must take these thoughts captive immediately and realize God never meant for her to be enslaved to servanthood, but to be empowered to lead by Godly example, which she does by serving through love and not guilt, condemnation or demand. Although the interaction with others in and of itself is harmless, she is often made to believe she cannot do so without having her motives questioned. She may know in her heart she is doing nothing wrong and that she is a good person, but the struggle with confidence from years of being made to feel like a "bad girl" still rages in her mind. The "bad girl" mentality is rooted in her from comments like:

> *"I see the way you talk to men"*
> *"They will think you are a prostitute"*
> *"Look at how you're dressed (sarcastically)"*
> *"You just have to be in the spotlight:*

Let me refer back to taking every thought captive for a moment. In your mind is where the battle rages. It is here that deception is planted and here that actions take root and begin to surface. These thoughts must be under submission if we are to break free from bondage.

"The tools of our trade aren't for market ing and manipulation, but they are for de-

molishing that entire massively corrupt culture. We use our powerful God-tools for smashing warped philosophies, tearing down barriers erected against the truth of God, fitting every loose thought and emotion and impulse into the structure of life shaped by Christ. Our tools are ready at hand for clearing ground of every obstruction and building lives of obedience into maturity."
2 Corinthians 10:4-6

Do you understand what that means for you daughter of Christ? Condemning thoughts, damaging emotions and impulses to react improperly are not in align with God's word and they must be put under subjection not being allowed to manipulate and control you. This battle can only be fought with the weapons of warfare Christ has given us. Truth, Righteousness (self-acceptance through who you are in Christ), Peace (in your spirit and testimony), Faith, Salvation, Prayer (continual) and Praise. We are told to be diligent, watching for these attacks which mean to steal, kill and destroy our purpose in life.

Returning once again to the captivity of isolation from others, especially in regards to the opposite sex, will keep you from developing any confidence in communicating with others. Communication is the only way we can win others for Christ. We must learn to insulate ourselves from negative influences, but never isolate ourselves from those we can help, whether male or female. Remember the woman at the well, Jesus did not allow the opinions of his disciples to stop Hs purpose of helping this woman. Others need your testimony and friendship as much as you need theirs. When well-meaning individuals offer this advice, it is perceived by the insecure woman as condemnation and continues her captivity. A woman who is confident in Christ will test this word for wisdom, not view it as condemnation. However, when jealousy rules in the accuser it becomes a captivity for a woman's ability to interact with others. The enemy uses the weakness of self-doubt in an insecure woman, which has been rooted in her for many years, to keep her confined to isolation and loneliness when her heart cries for love and acceptance. Satan knows that if he can keep her from feeling love, even in its purest forms, she will never able to love completely and further God's kingdom.

An isolated and insecure woman will have a greater battle raging inside her to be loved because love is the basis of life. Without it we cease to live and eventually die of loneliness. When the need for love is unmet by a spouse, a woman knows she is especially vulnerable and will often withdrawal even more from others, especially the opposite sex, for fear she might become what others have predetermined she already is. She will be inclined to comply with their wishes or threats and remain isolated in an attempt to satisfy them and restrain untrue rumors from running wild. Wisdom must be the basis for all her actions and decisions. Fear should never be the reason for decision making. Her need for love, friendship and interaction will keep her attempting to step out of isolation, but may also find her repeating this vicious cycle again and again because of her insecurity. In order to break free from this mental bondage women must walk in confidence not fear of what others will do, say or think, knowing her interaction with others (even the opposite sex) is not immoral, but part of being mortal. Freedom and purpose begin when a woman knows she is in the right and righteous through Christ, even when some declare otherwise. This is when the tears of loneliness meet wisdom and she begins to live a life free from the opinions of others and one based upon the truths of God. Does this mean she's perfect? Absolutely not! The quest for perfection is too big for any human being to carry. We know there never has been and never will be any perfect person, except Christ. The condemnation of others will often put undue stress to achieve perfection on a woman always ending in inner disappointment. When this goal of perfection is unobtainable, time and time again a woman faces two choices—self-discovery or self-defeat. For many it is met with self-defeat which becomes her reality. This inward defeat is a road which takes her to outward destruction, giving up her goals, accepting the behaviors of the world and becoming hard, calloused and emotionally destroyed. It comes to the surface in the way she talks, walks, dresses, what she does and where she goes. She finds no love in her journey of defeat, only more condemnation and judgment in response to her behavior. This leads many a defeated woman to mask her pain with drugs, alcohol and sex. Ultimately, her road ends in spiritual death, often contrib uting to a physical death. Thus the enemy has fulfilled his purpose to steal (her value), kill (her purpose) and destroy (her life.)

"The thief comes only in order to steal, kill and destroy. I came that they may have and enjoy life, and have it in abundance (to the full, till it overflows)"
John 10:10

Oh that the heart of this woman could be restored to righteousness by understanding she doesn't need to be perfect, but must accept the grace of her God.

"I can anticipate the response that is coming: "I know that all God's commands are spiritual, but I'm not. Isn't this also your experience?" Yes. I'm full of myself— after all, I've spent a long time in sin's prison. What I don't understand about

myself is that I decide one way, but then I act another, doing things I absolutely despise. So if I can't be trusted to figure out what is best for myself and then do it, it becomes obvious that God's command is necessary. But I need something more! For if I know the law but still can't keep it, and if the power of sin within me keeps sabotaging my best intentions, I obviously need help! I realize that I don't have what it takes. I can will it, but I can't do it. I decide to do good, but I don't really do it; I decide not to do bad, but then I do it anyway. My decisions, such as they are, don't result in actions. Something has gone wrong deep within me and gets the better of me every time. It happens so regularly that it's predictable. The moment I decide to do good, sin is there to trip me up. I truly delight in God's commands, but it's pretty obvious that not all of me joins in that delight. Parts of me covertly rebel, and just when I least expect it, they take charge. I've tried everything and nothing helps. I'm at the end of my rope. Is there no one who can do anything for me? Isn't that the real question? The answer, thank God, is that Jesus Christ can and does. He acted to set *things right in this life of contradictions where I want to serve God with all my heart and mind, but am pulled by the influence of sin to do something totally different."*

Romans 7:15-25

When good isn't good enough and better is not best, a woman will often be reduced to defeat in her mind, and left to remain, this defeat will eventually kill her heart. It is not perfection God is looking for, but a heart after His own. Paul states, "Thank God in Jesus Christ we can have a heart and mind for the things of God." David, knew this better than anyone. God favored David and blessed his life despite his affair with Bathsheba and his many failures because of his heart, confessed honesty, repentance and reverence for God. In order to walk out of the shadows, woman of God, it is not a perfect mind, a perfect body or perfect decisions, but a heart sold out to your God.

In regard to all of this I must say, decisions will always have consequences. David did not escape the consequences of his actions, but entered into the grace of

God through his repentant heart. When others object to or debate a woman's decision and find themselves unable to accept it, they must decide for themselves their own course of action. Individuals are given rule over their own beliefs, actions and thoughts. In the case of a woman standing up to a manipulative situation to gain her purpose, she may not find her companion's decisions favorable and the price she pays for her new-found individuality may be a hard one. It may result in abandonment and her blessing of purpose may come through raindrops and her healing may come through tears as it is so beautifully sung by Laura Story in the song "Blessings." One thing is sure and that is her discovery of freedom to be all she was created to be and experience will be worth the price she paid and Christ will reward her efforts to fulfill her purpose.

"...and He is the rewarder of those who earnestly and diligently seek Him out."

Hebrews 11:6

In closing let me encourage you of Christ's presence with you in your difficult journey, in your tears and fears.

"You've kept track of my every toss and turn through the sleepless nights, Each tear entered in your ledger, each ache written in your book."

Psalm 56:8

It is when a woman surrenders all she has and all she is, both positive and negative, to be all God has for her and sees in her that she has discovered wisdom.

May wisdom lead you out of the shadows of heartache and fear and into insight and understanding in the things God has planned for your life.

"That people may know skillful and Godly wisdom and instruction, discern and comprehend the words of understanding and insight."

Proverbs 1:2

Chapter 9

Praise To Plunder

"Jehoshaphat's Journey"

Many times it seems our faith is challenged over and over again. We are told to praise through our circumstances and continue the good fight. At times the battle seems much bigger than any we've faced and reasoning challenges our faith. We tend to look for worldly answers when we are fighting spiritual battles. The temptation to take control of our situations and react through reasoning becomes stronger than our ability to move in faith. I love the story of King Jehoshaphat. We can learn a lot from him to apply in our own lives during our battle with fear of moving forward.

We read the story of Jehoshaphat , king of Judah, in 2 Chronicles 20. Here a story of challenge unfolds as he is under attack by the Moabites, Ammonites and Meunites. They had united as a huge force and were on their way to fight him. It tells us that Jehoshaphat was shaken and looked to God for help as well as ordering a fast. He then took his position in front of his kingdom and prayed,

"O God, are you not God and ruler of all kingdoms below? You hold all power and

might in your fist; no one stands a chance against you. ...when the worst happens— whether war or flood or disease or famine, we take our place before this Temple (we know you are personally present in this place) and pray out our pain and trouble, we know that you will listen and give victory...and now they've come to kick us out of the country you gave us...Oh God, won't you take care of them? We're helpless before this vandal horde ready to attack us. We don't know what to do; we're looking to you."
2 Chronicles 20: 6-12

Have you ever felt like the enemy conspiring against you was three times your strength? Just as Jehoshaphat cried out to God and took his position, we must do the same if we want to walk in victory. Pouring out our fears and troubles, we must reaffirm God's ability to conquer. When you are battling for your God-given purpose, be assured the enemy will put up a great fight, but not so great that God can't lead you to victory. You don't always need to know what to do, but rather who will do it through you. Jehoshaphat did not know what he was going to do to protect what God had given him, but he did know God would show him. When you are at the end of your rope, there is more of God and His power at work.

"You're blessed when you're at the end of your rope. With less of you there is more of God and his rule."
Matthew 5:3

God responded to his request:

"Don't be afraid, don't pay an mind to this vandal horde. This is God's war, not yours. You won't have to lift a hand in this battle, just stand firm. Watch God's saving work for you take shape. Don't be afraid, don't waver. March out boldly tomorrow—God is with you. Believe firmly in God, your God and your lives will be firm. Believe in your prophets and you'll come out on top."
2 Chronicles 20:15-17, 20

Usually, our first response to stepping into our purpose is fear. Fear of the conflict it might cause, fear of spreading yourself too thin, fear of financial challenge, fear of failure, fear of change, etc.. Where God calls you he gets you. When God calls you to something He casts away your fear. Casting away fear does not mean you don't question how you can fulfill it, but rather that you know that God's ability is bigger than your doubt. Your job is to stand firm in your purpose and walk boldly toward your call, unwavering, knowing God is with you. Listen to the wisdom of those God has placed in your lives to encourage you forward. God always prepares the soldiers to stand with you and lead you to victory.

Jehoshaphat's response to God's answer was to face down in gratitude and worship. They took God at His word and praised as though the battle was over. When you face your battle, do you take God at His word to deliver the victory and praise Him as though you've reached the Promised Land? Or do you have a tendency to waver, taking small steps but holding back your praise till you see the victory? Jehoshaphat went even farther in his worship, engaging a choir to march ahead of the troops. As soon as they started praising, the ambush was set against the enemy and destroyed. The enemy became confused and the victory was won. Here is what happens when we follow this pattern of praise: Setting forth praise and speaking out victory as we walk toward the enemy and deal with the enemy confuses the enemy and his plans are uprooted. Think for a minute about a difficult situation you may be in in regards to a relationship with someone. If every verbal attack against you was met with a positive attitude and an inability to change your demeanor, would this not confuse the one attempting to stir up discord?

Next time you find yourself in a confrontation with someone, stop and remember the life of Jehoshaphat. Turn on your uplifting music, keep a sweet spirit, sing praise songs in your home and keep moving forward. The enemy will be beside himself trying to figure out how his planned backfired. Meanwhile, you will move on, move up and move out of the way the obstacles that were meant to stop your progress and steal your focus.

"Me" focus must become "He" focus

if we want to taste victory. We can give God all "WE" want, but until we give Him what "HE" wants we have done nothing and will not taste victory!

What does God want of you today? Trust in His ability to bring you through. This is the obedience he is looking for. Do you trust God with your life even when you don't understand what He's doing? The truth is He created your life for Him and you are a vessel He chooses to work through to bring glory to His name. If He believes in you, you must never quit believing in Him to accomplish all He wills for your life.

"God is the finisher of your faith and will bring to completion the good work He has started in you."
Philippians 1:6

Chapter 10

Progressing The Next Generation

"Schooling, Stabilizing
&
Securing"

One of the biggest desires and concerns of a woman is for the future of her children. For a single mother, she wonders if she can fill the void of her fatherless child and show enough love to give this child the security he or she needs. A married woman's desire is often much the same when she is in a marriage where the father is not actively involved in the lives of the children or when his interests take precedence over the needs of the children. The mother's natural instincts go into overdrive to fill the gaps of neglect or rejection the children might experience. In a separated or divorced woman this same instinct is actively striving to give the children a solid foundation of what God intended to be, yet helping them understand that sometimes things are not as they should be. Helping her children strive for excellence in God's eyes despite the imperfect situation in which they have found themselves is in the heart of a mother. Many young widowed women have the added challenge of comforting a child and being both mother and father while helping guard them from bitterness toward God for the loss of their father.

Let's talk about the mother who finds herself single-handedly raising her children for excellence. Many women take on the task of homeschooling the children, some with the hands-on support of their husbands and others with verbal support. This is especially difficult for those who only receive verbal support. Their tasks are as complex as that of a public school teacher. Often their authority is called into question. You are asked, "Why?" "Because I know what's best for your education," you reply, looking into the disapproving faces of your children. What makes these times especially challenging is when the father is not an active part of the children's schooling. A father who serves only as a disciplinarian, rather than someone who rewards accomplishment will not be respected, but feared. This fear becomes rebellion from children and only adds to the challenge a mother faces in bringing her children under submission. When mom is present the children will strive to express an independence that is not allowed in the presence of their father. A perfect balance in a perfect world would be as follows: the father comes home, asks the children how school was today, praises their A on a test and talks with them about any undesirable behavior. They should be the principal who issues the honor roll and serves detention. Unfortunately, not all women live in this perfect world. Many are acting as teacher, principal and mother. The children are left to decipher daily which role the mother is playing. At this point I must say that this is not because children are rebellious children, but rather because the perfect order of authority and balance of love is not present in the home.

Another area of disfunction in a home is in the "buying of the children's affections." Many times mother and father compete to "out-give" one another in regards to their children as an expression of love in competition to hold their favor. The children are always taught that love comes only through reward when the parents engage in this activity. This sets up a terrible pattern of rejection and expectation in the life of a child. This can be especially present in separated and divorced parents. A mother must guard her heart and refrain from participating in this behavior no matter how much she loves her children. The greatest love a mother can offer her child, even though it may seem unappreciated now, is a balanced and Christ-like love that secures their futures. These are the truths that will keep them stable when life throws challenge.

"For the moment all discipline seems painful rather than pleasant, but later it yields the peaceful fruit of righteousness to those who have been trained by it."
Hebrews 12:11

"Whoever spares the rod hates his son, but he who loves him is diligent to discipline him. "
Proverbs 13:24

"For whom the Lord loves He corrects, even as a father corrects the son in whom he delights."
Proverbs 3:12

Children will learn where their stability is through this type of parenting. Children long for the interaction with their parent as a means of acceptance and this is also found in discipline. For women who are the balance of both in the absence of a father's balance this will often seem un-rewarded and difficult. Behind the scenes this mother may work an extra job to provide for the children's daily needs while the father provides for his own and for the children's occasional pleasures. In the case of separated or divorced parents time spent at Dad's house may seem like a vacation with all the luxuries of toys, movies, pizza and fun. Coming home to mom may mean leftovers, routine and discipline, but it will always mean love. Understand this one fact—"Love is not materialistic, but spiritual." A mother who welcomes her child with a safe haven of happiness and steadfastness will be mother of the year and her children will learn to depend on this behavior as genuine. Luxuries provided by the absent parent will not override the genuine behavior of a caring parent. Those who place their worth in material things will be disappointed when life removes them down the road. Children will always return to the parent who stands on God's word when a difficulty arises because they understand that things cannot take away their pain or change their circumstance.

Moms, please take heart and know that although the tears are cried behind closed doors for the desire to give your children more, what you are giving is the best and God rewards those who diligently seek Him. Your work is not in vain.

"...my chosen ones will have satisfaction in their work. They won't work and have nothing come of it, they won't have children snatched out from under them. For they themselves are plantings blessed by God, with their children and grandchildren likewise God-blessed."
Isaiah 65:23

Put your heart at ease dear mother, for God has promised you profit from your efforts and stability for your children.

"And all your children shall be disciples [taught by the Lord and obedient to His will and great shall be the peace and undisturbed composure of your children."
Isaiah 54:13

I want to address another fear that married women commonly have as mothers and that is "the fear of abandonment."

Many women have been made to believe they are incapable of being a good mother, one the children can depend on when this is just not true. The efforts to demean a mother's love is an attempt to make her feel incapable of providing enough for the children, thus she fears abandonment and failure. We have already talked about fear as "false evidence appearing real," but how can a mother defeat this fear and disprove its credibility?

This woman may be working diligently, exhaustingly to provide the meals, have supper on the table nightly, prepare the lesson plans, work the part-time job, run a home business and even care for aging parents. Often her feats will be met with exhaustion, lack of support and comments intended to make her feel unbalanced and inadequate. She will often be disciplined for anything she buys for herself, making her feel guilty and pointing out her neglect to invest in something for the family. She might hear comments like this:

"You're neglecting the family"
"What you do is not benefitting us"
"You're so perfect (sarcastically)"

"The kids miss you"
"Where did you get that?"
"I am tired of eating this or that."
And the list goes on and on....

She may be required to work the part time job to alleviate financial burden, but not allowed to attempt other ventures of interest, even those she sees as future stability for her children, without being made to feel guilty. This will especially be present if she enjoys what she is doing and her spouse is dissatisfied in his career. These responses will often overwhelm the mother and seek to stop her from doing what she knows she has been called to do and make her feel unworthy. She may experience moments of panic and anxiety when her spouse pours on the kindness one day and the condemnation another. Restless nights of worry may begin to overtake her, as well as thoughts of how she can make it if her spouse abandons her. This thought pattern is a direct attack from the enemy and a woman must remember she has married her maker and He will never abandon her, forsake her or leave her destitute of provision.

"But God says, 'Even if a giant grips the plunder and a tyrant holds my people prisoner, I'm the one who's on your side, defending your cause, rescuing your children. And your enemies, crazed and desperate will turn on themselves killing each other in a frenzy of self-destruction."
Isaiah 49:25-26

Even at times when it seems all of her efforts are invested in the family and the reward is small while her spouse seeks to satisfy his position, career and material wants. Many times the husband believes he is investing in the family because he has allowed the family to participate in his pleasure. Although this quality of sharing is favorable, the heart behind the gift is often firstly focused on what he desires and secondly allowed for enjoyment by the family.

"So those who now are last will be first then, and those who now are first will be last then. For many are called, but few are chosen."
Matthew 20:16

God calls all to seek first the kingdom, but

many will seek their will first expecting to receive the kingdom. They will not be chosen.

"And Jesus called them to Him and said, 'You know that the rulers of the Gentiles lord it over them, and their great men hold them in subjection [tyrannizing over them]...Not so shall it be among you; but whoever wishes to be great among you must be your servant. And whoever desires to be first among you must be your slave—just as the Son of Man came not to be waited on but to serve, and to give His life as a ransom for many (the price paid to set them free.)"
Matthew 20:25-28

Mothers are capable of working, educating, and equipping their children to become mature young adults of focus and vision. They are able to do this because they themselves have been equipped with the guidance of the Holy Spirit and He directs the steps of the righteous. No one loves her children more than her God. The honorable life is often the road less traveled. Be of good cheer Woman of God, for your serving in sorrow will be rewarded with righteousness. 156

Chapter 11

Thistles Transformed Sequoias

"Rising Above the Winds of Turmoil & Taking Root."

In the previous chapters we have taken a look at how codependency, complacency and insecurity develops. We have viewed the signs and gone further by learning how to forgive those who have contributed to these problems. It matters not whether it was a spouse, friend, family member or coworker, all three of these problems can come about to steer us off course. One thing remains the same, we must forgive and remain rooted in love, taking our life of thistles and transforming it into a life of strength and stability like the sequoia. This is where our life begins to change course and we experience all God has for us as women.

"So you'll go out in joy, you'll be led into a whole and complete life. No more thistles, but giant sequoias….
Isaiah 55:12-13

To better understand why God used thistles and sequoias, we need to look at the characteristics of both. Most thistles have sharp prickles surrounding the flower bulb (the heart of the plant). Some are completely covered with these prickles as a defense mechanism to discourage animals from feeding on it. Thistles are easily carried by the wind where they will reproduce. They are a main attraction for insects and goldfinches often make their homes in the thistle. It is interesting to note that the goldfinch flies in wavy, stirring up motion drawing attention to itself. Has your life been conflicted and inhabited by a goldfinch? Insecure women can be an attraction on which others feed on to draw attention to themselves. These women will often put up a defense around their hearts as well as every part of their lives as a means to keep from getting hurt again. Their insecurity and instability make them easy targets for the goldfinch.

"Don't be naive. There are difficult times ahead. As the end approaches, people are going to be self-absorbed, money-hungry, self-promoting, stuck-up, profane, contemptuous of parents, crude, coarse, dog-eat-dog, unbending, slanderers, impulsively wild, savage, cynical, treacherous, ruthless, bloated windbags, addicted to lust, and allergic to God. They'll make a show of religion, but behind the scenes they're animals. Stay clear of these

people. These are the kind of people who smooth-talk themselves into the homes of unstable and needy women and take advantage of them; women who, depressed by their sinfulness, take up with every new religious fad that calls itself "truth."

2 Timothy 3:1-7

As women, we must stand tall and embrace our value in Christ or we will allow condemnation of our imperfections and others words become a false truth for our lives. It is crucial for women who have a history of insecurity to discover their value before they attempt new relationships or they will be carried by the wind of untruth again finding themselves repeating this cycle.

It is very easy for women in these types of relationships to grasp at any signs of change and be deceived. When the pressure subsides, the purpose does too. When the wind stops blowing don't stop going and growing or you will never achieve the call God has for your life.

"But when Pharaoh saw that there was

temporary relief, he made his heart stubborn and hard and would not listen or heed as the Lord had said."
Exodus 8:15

Do not be afraid to push on to becoming your sequoia. God will instruct you step by step along the path for your life and walking it out in faith.

"I am the One comforting you. What are you afraid of—or who? And here you are quaking like an aspen before the tyrant who thinks he can kick down the world. But what will come of the tantrums? The victims will be released before you know it. They're not going to die. They're not even going to go hungry. I teach you how to talk word by word and personally watch over you."
Isaiah 51;12-16

Arise woman of God, for it is time to take root and stop letting the winds of continual turmoil toss you to and fro. It is time to wake up to reality, get to your feet, fix yourself up, dust off the depression and fear and throw off the chains of bondage. You are an heir of the king. The heir does not wallow in self-pity and fear, but walks boldly with her King. She knows her worth and walks in confidence.

"Wake up, wake up! Pull on our boots..Dress up in your Sunday best...Those who want no part of God have been culled out. They won't be coming along. Brush off the dust and get to your feet, captive Jerusalem. Throw off your chains, captive daughter.."
Isaiah 52:1-2

The pain of broken marriages, friendships and relationships can leave an emptiness that overtakes not only the inner man, but the outer man as well. Depression will cause you to sleep long, deny destiny and quit trying to look your best. A "give up" mentality sets in when a woman does not understand her value. God has words for this woman in regard to the pain she has suffered and the direction she has lost.

"Clear lots of ground for your tents. Make your tents large. Spread out. Think big! Use plenty of rope, drive the tent pegs deep. You're going to need lots of elbow

room for your growing family."
Isaiah 54:2

God desires you to prepare for the future He is getting ready to give you. Up until now you may have struggled, doubted and despaired. Get ready, think big! You don't serve a God of limitations, but a God that does beyond what you can think or dare to dream. Don't hold back out of fear. Your humiliations and hurts of those you have loved so deeply will be forgotten. If you have been an abandoned wife, emotionally, physically, or economically, God is replacing your troubled past and present with a promised future. Go out with joy into the new life God has prepared for you, be led into completeness. You are no longer a thistle, but a giant sequoia.

"No test or temptation that comes your way is beyond the course of what others have had to face. All you need to remember is that God will never let you down; he'll never let you be pushed past your limit; he'll always be there to help you come through it."
1 Corinthians 10:13

Are you ready to make the transformation into a sequoia? Let's examine now the characteristics of the sequoia. Sequoias are commonly known as coast redwood trees, the world's largest tree. They can grow to a height of 279 feet and measure 26 feet wide. They have an incredible life span of up to 3500 years. Interestingly enough, they have a built-in fire protection within their bark made of thick, fibrous and furrowed wood. With this system in place fire does not generally kill them, but just removes competing thin bark which aids in regeneration. The leaves of this monstrous tree are evergreen. Sequoias have the ability to sprout new life from a lost or broken branch or one destroyed by fire. I hope you are getting a picture of what God sees within your life. You are considered strong, magnificent and able to conquer this life. The turmoil and stress that come against you are blocked out by your unique defense system in Christ. He has toughened you with a 3 strand cord not easily broken. You are not alone!

"And one standing alone can be attacked and defeated, but two can stand back-to-

back and conquer; three is even better, for a triple-braided cord is not easily broken."
Ecclesiastes 4:12

Your ability for re-growth after brokenness, the fire of anger and hatred and lost love is assured. New life can and does begin after devastation. Peace will be reinstated in your life.

"....I'm promising now no more anger, no more dressing you down....My love won't walk away from you, my covenant commitment of peace won't fall apart. The God who has compassion on you says so."
Isaiah 54:9-10

Though she may fall down she will not stay down.

"For there is hope for a tree, if it be cut down, that it will sprout again, and that its shoots will not cease "
Job 14:7

The woman of God will be well rooted near her source of life (Christ) fearing no raging fires, ever green, anxious for nothing, cared for in the hard times and never without increase.

"For he shall be like a tree planted by the waters that spreads out its roots by the river; and it shall not see and fear when heat comes; but its leaf shall be green. It shall not be anxious and full of care in the year of drought, nor shall it cease yielding fruit."
Jeremiah 17:8

Loneliness will have no place in the sequoia woman of God. She will be strong, able to rebuild, restore and renovate her life and the world she lives in.

"I will always show you where to go, I'll give you a full life in the emptiest of places—firm muscles, strong bones….You'll use the old rubble of past lives to build anew, rebuild the foundations from out of your past. You'll be known as those who can fix anything, restore old ruins, rebuild and renovate, make the community livable again."
Isaiah 58:11-12

The regrets of the past that trouble

your future will be put to rest for Christ will bring to completion what He has promised.

"You'll get a brand-new name straight from the mouth of God. You shall also be [so beautiful and prosperous as to be thought of as] a crown of glory and honor in the hand of the Lord, and a royal diadem [exceedingly beautiful] in the hand of your God. No more will anyone call you Rejected and your country will no more be called Ruined...because God delights in you...Tell the daughter Zion, 'Look! Your Savior comes, ready to do what he said he'd do, prepared to complete what he promised.' Zion will be called new names: Holy People,, God-Redeemed, Sought Out, City Not Forsaken."
Isaiah 62:2-4, 11-12

"So shall My word be that goes forth out of My mouth: it shall not return to Me void [without producing any effect, useless], but it shall accomplish that which I please and purpose, and it shall prosper in the thing for which I sent it."
Isaiah 55:11

Get ready! The thistle is no more and the sequoia has taken its place. Grab hold of your purpose, stand tall and step into your victory!

Chapter 12

When God Gives Love

"Letting Love Find You"

Our faith can be reinstated, our purpose made plain, our prosperity abundant, our wisdom increased and our devotion unending, but without love we have nothing and are nothing. Love is the central need and the greatest gift mankind can have and give. Without it we strive for happiness to no avail. With it we live life to the fullest.

"We, though, are going to love—love and be loved. First we were loved, now we love. He loved us first."
1 John 4:19

It is a force no man can explain, but no man can deny. Love is the wardrobe of God that clothes your life with happiness.

"So, chosen by God for this new life of love, dress in the wardrobe God picked out for you: compassion, kindness, humility, quiet strength, discipline. Be even-tempered, content with second place, quick to forgive an offense. Forgive as quickly and completely as the Master forgave you. And regardless of what else you put on, wear love. It's your basic, all-purpose garment. Never be without it."

Colossians 3:12-14

The single woman longs for it, the married woman flourishes in it, the separated woman is confused by the lack of it, the divorced woman is hurt by it, the widowed woman understands it.

"Love never gives up"
"Love cares more for others than self"
"Love doesn't want what it doesn't have"
"Love doesn't strut"
"Love doesn't have a swelled head"
"Love doesn't force itself on others"
"Love isn't always 'me first'"
"Love doesn't fly off the handle"
"Love doesn't keep score of the sins of others"
"Love doesn't revel when others grovel"
"Love takes pleasure in the flowering of truth"
"Love puts up with anything"
"Love trusts God always"
"Love always looks for the best"
"Love never looks back"
"Love keeps going to the end"
"Love never dies"
1 Cor. 13:4-8

The journey you're on may be full of love or scarred by love. The woman whose life is surrounded by love has found the secret to happiness. The woman who is still waiting for love, she won't be disappointed. Her heart must pursue her God and love will pursue her in turn.

"Be anxious for nothing, but in everything by prayer and supplication, with thanksgiving, let your requests be made known to God; and the peace of God, which surpasses all understanding, will guard your hearts and minds through Christ Jesus."
Philippians 4:6

The fear of loneliness must not be allowed to rule her spirit, for in its arms she meets confusion, disappointment and distraction from her purpose. Her vision is clouded by her longing and her feelings overcome by her hurting. Fear, if left in place will be manifested in hasty decisions which will lead you away from God's best.

"There is no fear where love exists. Rather, perfect love banishes fear, for fear involves punishment, and the person

who lives in fear has not been perfected
in love."
1 John 4:18

"So this is my prayer: that your love will
flourish and that you will not only love
much but well. Learn to love appropri-
ately. You need to use your head and test
your feelings so that your love is sincere
and intelligent, not sentimental gush."
Philippians 1:9-10

One of the hardest things we do as humans is waiting. We live in a world of instant gratification and look for it as a lost treasure. We often search desperately for what we want, but occasionally for what we need. Many women find themselves searching and searching for love only to find themselves back in the same relationships that left them unloved before. Others who have never experienced love often move ahead of God and sacrifice His best for them.

"Oh, let me warn you, sisters in Jerusa-
lem: Don't excite love, don't stir it up, un-
til the time is ripe—and you're ready."
Song of Solomon 8:4

To be ready in body is not an indicator of heartfelt readiness. Someone once said, "God answers your longing in three ways:"

"He says yes and gives you what you want"
"He says no and gives you something better"
"He says wait and gives you the best"

"Wait for the Lord; be strong, and let your heart take courage; wait for the Lord! "
Psalm 27:14

The reward of love is sure for those whose hearts trust and wait upon their God. They will find strength in His promises and peace in His presence. No one can out- give Him!

"For since the world began no one has seen or heard of such a God as ours, who works for those who wait for him!"
Isaiah 64:4

We have always been taught to plan and set goals looking toward the future in expectation. We instill this in our children and we enforce it in our lives. However, it can be overemphasized when it comes to relationships. We can set time sensitive goals in business, education, etc... But, when it comes to love, we must let God control the timing. We must remove our daily focus of "happiness someday, somewhere with someone" and replace it with "right now, right here and right with God" thinking. This is not easy for a woman with a codependent history. She must be reprogrammed in her mind to discover her future. Coming out of a codependent relationship is especially challenging in that she is learning to stand up for her beliefs while discovering what they are at the same time. She is learning who she is in a world she's never seen. It is crucial for her to fall in love with her Lord to develop strength as she walks out her independence and prepares her heart to love again. She may be plagued by a fear of not being accepted for who she is in new relationships. Finding someone who will build her up and not tear her down becomes the longing of her heart.

"Trust in the LORD with all your heart and lean not on your own understanding; in

all your ways acknowledge him, and he will make your paths straight."
Proverbs 3:5-6

Someone once said, *"God didn't give you the strength to get back on your feet so that you could run back to the same thing that knocked you down."* Now that you are learning who you are and stepping out of the shadows of codependency, complacency and insecurity you must never allow yourself to waste God's grace. In Him you have been made and with Him you will find true love. Hold your mind in a state of undistracted attention. We must be reminded daily of this importance.

"My dear friends, this is now the second time I've written to you, both letters reminders to hold your minds in a state of undistracted attention."
2 Peter 3:1

God is on the scene even when He's unseen!

"Clearly you are a God who works behind the scenes."
Isaiah 45:15

ABOUT THE AUTHOR

Ann Haney is a specialist in the field of women empowerment, saving money and self-starting your own business. Her first published book, The Homeschool Daily Planner For Curriculum became a 5 year running best seller and continues to excel in residual income yearly. Along with Aaron Publishing, Ann is the CEO of Living In Abundance and founder of Ann Haney Ministries and Coaching Purpose Restoration. In 2012 Ann released her book entitled, "Exploding Into Successful Entrepreneurship, telling her story and teaching people the steps to discovering their talent & using it for a successful career. It has become a great success through her financial empowerment teachings and supplemental financial empowerment workbook. In addition to homeschooling her children for over 18 years, Ann has taught thousands of people across the nation to save thousands of dollars a year and become self-made entrepreneurs who excel at being all God created them to be. Ann travels extensively helping people discover their hidden skills and apply them and change their lives from victims of circumstances to overcoming achievers of success. Ann is an ordained minister and helps others discover the truths in God's word that lead to a happy, successful and productive life. Ann counsels many women in the following areas:

- Parenting
- Career Development
- Personal Growth
- Homeschooling
- Business Start Up
- Time Management
- Health
- Couponing

Her experience can help you:
- Discover your strengths
- Transform your weaknesses
- Implement your ideas
- Set goals

- Stay focused
- Step out of insecurity, complacency, and codependency
- Initiate forward progress
- Build your network
- Build your confidence
- Identify obstacles
- Discover your God-given gift
- Be accountable
- Develop written business Correspondence

Ann's biography—

*Radio appearances:

Renee Bobb Empowerment For Women Radio Talk Show
Devon O'Day Plain Jane Wisdom Radio Talk Show
Common $ense-The Money Show Talk Radio at Fisk University
The Patrenna Singletary Empowerment Virtual Teleconference &
Talk Radio (behalf of TN Proprietary Business School Association)

*Newspaper Coverage:

Tennessean, Nashville, TN
Leaf Chronicle, Clarksville, TN
Daily News Journal, Murfreesboro, TN
Times Gazette, Shelbyville, TN (columnist in 2011)
Upside of Money "Faith & Finance"
Nashville Examiner, Nashville, TN (columnist)
Illinois Alliant
Lebanon Democrat (columnist 2012-Present)

*Media Coverage:

Nashville's Fox 17 News with Stacy Case
Channel 19 Nashville Perfect Peace Unlimited with Sylvia Page

*Speaking Portfolio:

State of Arkansas Farm Bureau 2011 convention for the Young Farmer's & Ranchers of Arkansas
State of TN 32nd Annual TAFCE Conference (TN Association for Family & Community Education)
Annual Nashville Women Empowerment Conferences
Fort Campbell Armed Services Ft. Campbell, KY

Daymar Institute (Clarksville, TN & Murfreesboro, TN)
Middle TN Goodwill Career Solution Centers (several locations)
UT Extension Offices in TN (several locations)
Southeast Homeschool Expo in Atlanta, GA
Alabama Homeschool Expo in Montgomery, AL
NSRO (National Self Reliance Expo, Denver, CO & Arlington, TX)
Chicago Homeschool Expo (2012)
Austin Peay State University
Bethel University (Nashville, TN)
Annual Every Woman's Expo (Lebanon, TN & Mt. Juliet, TN)
State of TN Rehabilitation Center
State of TN Alvin C. York VA Recovery Center
State of TN EFNEP (Expanded Food & Nutrition Education Program)
Nonprofits/Churches/Schools/Government Organizations/ County Fairs/Businesses

Note From The Author

My prayer for you is that God reveals His purpose for your life and shows you how valuable you are to Him. I pray blessing, prosperity and fulfillment on your life as you step out of the shadows. May you always be abundant in wisdom, direction and confidence bringing glory to God and a witness to others of His love for His people.

If you do not know my God I invite you to give your heart to Him today. Say this prayer and start experiencing a new and complete life.

"Lord, I know I have broken your laws and my sins have separated me from you. I am sorry and I want to turn away from my past sinful life. Please forgive me. I believe your son, Jesus Christ died for my sins, was resurrected from the dead, is alive, and hears my prayer. I ask you to become Lord of my life, to rule and reign in my heart. Please help me obey You, and do Your will for the rest of my life. In Jesus' name I pray, Amen."

www.ingramcontent.com/pod-product-compliance
Lightning Source LLC
Chambersburg PA
CBHW052002090426

42741CB00008B/1510